FAMOUS REGIMENTS

The Dorset Regiment

FAMOUS REGIMENTS

Edited by

Lt.-General Sir Brian Horrocks

The Dorset Regiment

(The 39th/54th Regiment of Foot)

by Hugh Popham

Leo Cooper Ltd., London

First published in Great Britain, 1970
by Leo Cooper Ltd.,
196 Shaftesbury Avenue, London W.C.2

Copyright © 1970 by Hugh Popham

Introduction Copyright © 1970 by
Lt.-General Sir Brian Horrocks

ISBN 0 85052 048 7

Made and printed in Great Britain by
Thomas Nelson (Printers) Ltd.,
London and Edinburgh

The Dorset Regiment

INTRODUCTION
by Lt.-General Sir Brian Horrocks

I knew and admired The Dorsets during the last War, but it was not until I read this short History, brilliantly compiled by Hugh Popham, that I realised quite how much the regiment had contributed to the expansion of the British Empire.

This book deserves an honoured place on bookshelves throughout one of the most beautiful counties in Britain, for it is a story of which anyone who has ever lived in Dorset will indeed be proud. Popham has done his work so well that there is little point in my delving into past history, except to draw attention to a few remarkable incidents which fall outside the almost set pattern we have come to expect from all our regular infantry regiments during ths last 250 years.

The Dorsets spent many years in Gibraltar, the West Indies and India. They are justly proud of their victory in India during the battle of Plassey in June, 1757 which, in the author's words, turned 'the English in India from a mercantile to a colonial administration'. Here they won a unique battle honour and the right to call themselves *Primus in Indus*. Plassey Day is still celebrated annually in the regiment.

Unlike most regiments, the Dorsets have a second Regimental Day to celebrate, the capture of Fort Marabout by the 54th (second battalion) in 1801. This was the key to Alexandria in Egypt and marked the first major defeat suffered by Napoleon's French Revolutionary Army.

Like many other regiments, they did their stint as Marines, and took part in a famous sea saga in 1857 when the *Sarah Sands* transport conveying the 54th Foot to India caught fire. The foreign crew took to the boats and the ship was saved by the gallant efforts of the soldiers.

Repeatedly throughout their history they became involved in maintaining order in Ireland, and it is a curious fact that on each occasion a number of Irish enlisted in the Regiment. The 54th landed in Ireland in 1798 a mere 150 strong and left two years later with 1,250 serving officers and men.

Let me now turn to the last war. Before dealing with my own experiences with the Dorsets I must mention the gallant conduct of the 2nd Battalion during the battle of Kohima, probably the second bloodiest battle of the war (the bloodiest was unquestionably Stalingrad). The battle raged for three weeks round the District Commissioner's bungalow and tennis court, with the Jap front line never more than fifty yards away. 'A' Company held on for a week under appalling conditions; the stench of the unburied dead is something which no one who fought in this vicious battle will ever forget. When 'A' Company was finally relieved only 28 of the original 100 Dorsets returned.

On August 1, 1944, after 14 months in hospital, I was flown out in Field-Marshal Montgomery's aircraft to take over command of 30 Corps on the Normandy Beaches. My first task was to visit all the battalions in my new Corps—three of these were Dorsets. The first battalion formed part of the 231 (First) Malta Brigade, then serving with the veteran 50th Division. They could proudly claim to have been the first troops ashore at Le Hamel on the Normandy Beaches on D Day, and this was their third assault-landing within twelve months—the previous two had been in Sicily and Italy, surely a record for any unit. Although they had been involved in hard fighting ever since the landing I found them in very good shape, with their morale quite

unshaken. They were subsequently attached to the Guards
Armoured Division during that rapid 250 mile armoured
advance made by 30 Corps, which ended six days later in
Brussels. The wonderful reception shown to *Les Liberateurs*
by the French villagers en route must have been some
compensation for the gruelling fighting on the beachheads.
This was probably the only time the British had been really
popular with the French.

The other two battalions were the 4th and 5th, and
formed part of the 43rd Wessex Division with its famous
Wyvern sign. When the territorial army was doubled in
April, 1939 the 4th Battalion had to form a duplicate, the
5th, which it did in the summer of 1939. The county was
divided in half for T.A. purposes. The 4th, with its Headquarters in Dorchester, represented Bridport and the
north of the county, while the 5th was based at Poole and
represented the south-eastern part.

I always maintain that the 43rd Wessex was the best-
trained division in the British Army on D Day. They led
the break-out from Normandy and carried out an intricate
and bitterly opposed river-crossing over the Seine at
Vernon. They subsequently joined my Corps again for the
Arnhem operation and the word 'Dorset' will always be
associated in my mind with the bitter fighting on the banks
of the Neder Rhine.

On September 25, 1944, I carried out a reconnaissance
from the top of Driel Church, as repeated efforts to
establish firm contact with the 1st British Airborne Division,
beleaguered by superior German forces on the North
Bank, had failed. This was largely because the Germans
dominated the river from high ground on either side and
crossing was a murderous business in face of their machine-
gun fire. The danger was that the airborne division might
well get cut off completely from the banks of the river, if
reinforcements did not arrive. I ordered General Thomas,
commanding the 43rd Division, to send over at least one

battalion that night. I promised him the support of the complete corps artillery.

When I returned, at 10 a.m. next day, from a meeting with the Second Army Commander, I found a very gloomy atmosphere awaiting me. About 300 men of the 4th Dorsets had crossed under annihilating fire but all communications with them had now ceased. I learned afterwards that they held on grimly for thirty-six hours and I am certain that this very gallant battalion had a lot to do with the fact that on the next night we managed to evacuate some 2,400 paratroops to the south bank. Alas, very few of the 4th made that nightmare return trip.

Subsequently, the remnants of the 4th and 5th battalions had some very hard fighting to maintain their positions on the South Bank.

From then on, we were together right up to the end of the War, which involved that extremely unpleasant Reichswald Battle—the crossing of the Rhine—the capture of Bremen, and my last sight of them was marching smartly past me during the Victory Parade at Bremerhaven after the Germans had surrendered.

The Dorsets had certainly contributed their part to the successful conclusion of the last Great War.

I will end this Introduction by quoting a paragraph of Hugh Popham's:

'The figures for the 54th in India after the first Burma War give the picture . . . with an average daily sick list of between 50–100. Against the names of many of those who died the entry read "*Worn out man* . . . due to be discharged". Those who are quick to decry Britain's imperial past tend to forget the price that was paid for it in life and health.'

How right he is.

Acknowledgements

I received much help and kindness while writing this history of The Dorsets, but I would particularly like to thank Major-General G. N. Wood, CB, CBE, DSO, MC, formerly Colonel of the Regiment, whose recollections of the First World War, *inter alia*, were invaluable; Brigadier A. E. C. Bredin, DSO, MC, DLL, who went to endless trouble to set the record straight; Lt.-Colonel O. G. W. White, DSO, MBE, Archivist and former curator of the Regimental Museum; Lt.-Colonel D. W. W. Wakely, MC, the present curator, and his staff in the Keep at Dorchester; and, as always, Mr. King and the staff of the Ministry of Defence Library.

Chapter

I

The 39th: 1702–1754

THE opening years of the eighthteenth century have an air of destiny about them. In 1701 James II died after thirteen years of exile, and the ragged banner of the Jacobite cause passed to his son whom Louis XIV promptly, and provocatively, recognised as James III of England. In Spain the throne left empty by the death of the necrophiliac Carlos II became the prize of rival claimants; and, since Louis chose to support his own grandson, Philip, Duke of Anjou, England supported the Habsburg Archduke Charles. William III, at war once more with France, was thrown from his horse at Hampton Court and died a month later. England had a queen again, and the command of her armies went to the greatest soldier of his age. England herself, after the political and religious upheavals of half a century, was beginning to assume a new and firmer stance.

With war the army needed men; and one of William's last acts before he died in March 1702 was to sign the commission establishing the 39th Regiment of Foot, to be raised by Colonel Richard Coote, formerly Lieutenant-Colonel of Lisburne's Foot. The establishment of the new Regiment was 40 officers and nearly 700 NCOs and men; and the green facings of their scarlet coats led to them, in time, being nicknamed the Green Linnets.

They were raised in Ireland on February 13, but within a year Colonel Coote was dead, killed in a duel with the scapegrace Lord Mohun; and four years later, under Colonel Nicholas Sankey, they sailed for Portugal. The campaign to support Charles, begun with such panache by the erratic Earl of Peterborough, had come to grief at the battle of Almanza. The 39th were not present, being still at Cork, awaiting passage: thus, the story that they—like the 13th with whom they fought at La Caya two years later, and whom Peterborough had put upon horses before Almanza—fought at that battle mounted, and so acquired the sobriquet of 'Sankey's Horse', is apocryphal.

The 39th's first action in Spain was, in fact, La Caya, in 1709, and it was a disaster. The English commander, the Earl of Galway, with 3,000 English and 9,000 Portuguese met 5,000 Spanish horse and 10,000 Spanish infantry, commanded by the Duke of Berwick (James II's bastard and a nephew of the Duke of Marlborough), on the banks of the River Caya near Badajoz. As at Almanza, the Portuguese cavalry broke and fled at the first French attack, and only the steadiness of Sankey's saved them during the retreat that followed. Colonel Sankey himself was captured, and remained a prisoner for more than three years.

It was the 39th's first battle on Spanish soil during the War of the Succession, and their last; and after the Treaty of Utrecht in 1713, and the cutback inevitable after a long war, they were in dire danger of being 'broke'; but were reprieved and sent to Gibraltar instead.

Certain threads of service run through the history of most of the line regiments in the eighteenth and nineteenth centuries: Ireland and Gibraltar are two. A third, less common, but one which binds the 39th and the 54th, was service with the Navy as Marines. The 39th had been transferred to Minorca when Admiral George Byng (father of another Admiral Byng, whose associations with the island were less fortunate) called there with his squadron in 1718 and hauled them on shipboard. A week later he brought a sizeable Spanish fleet to battle off Cape Passaro,* and in a running fight involving a series of single ship and

---

* Early on July 10, 1943, the 1st Dorsets landed at Marzamemi, immediately north of Cape Passaro.

ship duels at close quarters the soldiers were kept busy. Among the Spanish ships destroyed was the *Volante* which fell to the *Montagu* with two companies of the 39th aboard.

After nearly a year at sea Byng sent them back to England to help meet a Spanish invasion threat; and when this, like that earlier Armada, was dispersed by gales, the Regiment were sent, for the second time in twenty years, to Ireland, to spend the next six years in relative peace and obscurity.

Then in 1726, with a fresh war against an Austro-Spanish entente brewing, the two earlier themes recur: the summer at sea once more, as Marines; and that winter, back to Gibraltar. According to the custom of the time they were known as Newton's, after their current colonel; and it was as Newton's that they settled down early in 1727 to withstand the second major attempt by the Spanish in twenty-three years to recover Gibraltar.

The bombardment and counter-bombardment; the gradual pushing forward of the Spanish lines across the isthmus; the rain and the heat; the food and drink scarce, bad and dear; the claustrophobia relieved by occasional convoys with supplies and reinforcements; the occasional danger from enemy artillery and musket-fire, and the closer and more real danger of their own guns blowing up: all these went on for five months without anything significant being achieved. On May 21, as if in desperation, the besiegers kept up 'a perfect storm of fire all day': a week later, the besieged retaliated by hitting their main magazine. Three weeks after that the siege petered out; and another desultory eighteenth-century war was over.

It was three years before the Regiment was relieved; but they could count themselves lucky; later they were to do fourteen years on the Rock without a break, and even this was not exceptional. In some ways, however, their next move was worse—to that White Man's Grave of the eighteenth century, the West Indies. In six months of very slight and random skirmishing against insurgent negroes in Jamaica, the 39th lost one-third of their strength from 'Yellow Jack' and cheap rum. And yet in 1732, when they were due for posting home, no less than 150 men from the 39th and the 34th took up the offer of £10, a free grant of land and slaves, transfer to the island's Independent Companies, and free passage for their families, and so joined the planters, pirates, deserters—and Monmouth's vanquished of Sedgemoor—that composed the young colony's European population. The rest, with John Cope as Colonel—later to be courtmartialled but acquitted after Prestonpans—recrossed the Atlantic for yet another spell in Ireland.

This time they were there twelve years, during which time they ran through a succession of Colonels. Few stayed long: none was noteworthy. Of more general interest, it was while they were there that, in 1740, the first Official Army List was issued; while eleven years later it was decreed that the 'Great Union' Colour should replace the Colonel's personal one. Although for some years yet regiments were still known by the name of their Colonel, the order of precedence initiated by James II in 1685 was firmly settled, and numbers gradually replaced the older title. It was all of a part with the evolution of the army under the Hanoverians by which regiments steadily ceased being the private preserve of their colonels, and were put on a more formal footing.

Apart from the fiasco of the amphibious operation against L'Orient in 1746, in which no unit involved distinguished itself, the Regiment saw little active service during the War of the Austrian Succession, and that little at sea again, with Hawke in a brisk action against a French fleet and convoy off Cape Ortegal. By 1748 they were back in Ireland. Four years later their Colonel, Richbell, departed to the 17th Foot, and his place was taken by a cantankerous veteran of the War of the Spanish Succession, John Adlercron.

Colonel John Adlercron (1680–1766), who commanded the 39th when the Regiment was 'Primus in Indis', and remained Colonel until his death.

Adlercron, of Swiss extraction, was over 60 when he came to the 39th; and he proved to be an archetypal Blimp, quite without imagination and a fearful stickler. But an impartial fate has bestowed on him a kind of immortality. If it was in spite of, rather than because of him, that the 39th achieved its first solid claim to fame, the fact remains that he was their Colonel when, in 1754, they were ordered to the support of 'the United Company of Merchants trading to the East Indies', and his name is indissolubly linked with theirs. His instructions were 'to repair forthwith to the East Indies with the regiment under your command'; and to that end the Regiment mustered at Kinsale in the blustery month of March 1754.

Chapter
2
The 39th: 1754–1757

SEVERAL matters delayed their departure. Gales damaged two of the convoy, and a stowaway was discovered aboard one of the ships. 'A demand to see her bosom', Major John Corneille records, 'obliged the poor creature to acknowledge that she had disguised herself in expectation of accompanying her husband . . . It was her misfortune', he adds drily, 'that the sexes are too easily distinguishable'. With twenty shillings raised by a whip-round, she was put tearfully ashore.

These hazards overcome, the fleet, commanded by Admiral Watson, set sail before 'a brisk gale from the north-east' at the end of March, and reached Madras five months later—to run straight into trouble. Not initially from the French or their Indian allies but from the East India Company who had asked for them to be sent, and whose own troops were under instructions from home to be placed under Adlercron's command.

It was an odd situation. The Company was a trading organisation with three main bases, known as factories, at Madras, Calcutta and Bombay; but it had been driven into certain limited military operations partly by its own greed and partly by the conflicting greed of others, most notably the French, which had led to friction with the native rulers. When the 39th arrived, however, there was a lull in the hostilities. This lasted for eighteen months; until, in fact, May 1756, when the Neronian young Siraj-ud-daula succeeded as Nawab of Bengal, and resolved to deal with these intrusive and interfering English merchants once and for all. He took by treachery the insignificant fort of

Cossimbazar, and, a fortnight later, by sheer weight of numbers, Calcutta. His European prisoners—146 of them—he incarcerated for the night in the 18 by 14-foot cell known to subsequent history as the Black Hole of Calcutta, from which 23 emerged next morning.

As soon as the news filtered through to Madras an expedition was planned, and Colonel Robert Clive of the Company was given command. This, needless to say, incensed old Adlercron, who refused to allow the Regiment to embark. The only members of the 39th who sailed for the Hugli on October 16, 1756, therefore, were three companies—276 men—who were already serving as Marines in Admiral Watson's squadron. They were commanded by Captains Grant, Weller and Eyre Coote, the last a descendant of the Regiment's first Colonel. He had been courtmartialled for his part in the Battle of Falkirk ten years before, 'broke', cleared, reinstated and promoted; his part in the campaign that followed suggests that his earlier vindication, though he was only twenty-one at Falkirk, was fully justified.*

It took Admiral Watson six weeks to beat the 400 miles from Madras to Fulta against the monsoon, a tedious voyage rendered miserable by heavy seas, hunger and scurvy. As soon as the first ships arrived Clive set off by land against the Nawab's new fort at Budge-Budge, 20 miles below Calcutta, while the ships sailed up river to support him. On arrival the 39th were put ashore, and Coote quickly took two of the outer forts. He was specifically ordered not to attack the main fort, while Clive went aboard the flagship to confer with Watson. However, a sailor by the name of Strachan, emboldened by arrack, took it upon himself to tackle it singlehanded, his mates went

---

* Coote later left the 39th, raised the 84th for Indian Service in 1759, but was appointed C-in-C of the Military Forces in Bengal, and later of all our forces in India. After an outstanding career he died, as Lt-General, in 1783, the victor of Wandewash (1760) and Porto Novo (1781).

to his assistance, and Budge-Budge fell for the price of four wounded.

With Budge-Budge demolished, the expedition continued up river, and early in the new year Clive recaptured Calcutta—a success which led to a sharp tiff with Coote, who had assumed command on Watson's orders. Calcutta was in English hands again; but Clive was after the Nawab; so, leaving Roger Drake, the Governor, and his Council to the congenial task of recovering their private property—'the only object which takes up the attention of the Bengal gentlemen', as Clive acidly observed—the expedition set off once more. They had not got far, however, before two things happened: Siraj-ud-daula advanced on Calcutta with 40,000 men, 40 guns and 50 elephants; and Clive received the news that England and France were once more at war.

The second of these two factors meant that the French at Chandernagore would have to be taken into account: the first led to a curious and inconclusive affray with the Nawab on the outskirts of Calcutta in which Clive's intended attack was disrupted by fog, which lifted at an inconvenient moment; only some smart work by Ensign Yorke in saving one of the little army's few guns enabled Clive to break up the Nawab's cavalry and cause that shifty potentate to retire and consider coming to terms.

His sincerity was considerably in doubt—he was, in fact, playing a double game with the French—and Clive marched on Chandernagore. On March 12 Coote and the 39th's Grenadiers opened the attack with spirit and took and held a number of the outlying batteries, while the *Tyger*, *Kent* and *Salisbury* were with difficulty brought up river and started to bombard the main citadel. In the duel that followed, *Kent* had 120 casualties and was damaged beyond repair, and *Tyger* had 80 killed and wounded; but the fire was too hot for the French Governor, who 'ordered the drum to beat a parley' at noon.

The stage was now cleared for a final reckoning with the

Nawab; but first there was three months of intrigue
between Clive, the Nawab and his disaffected subjects, the
outcome of which was an arrangement—not the last the
British were to make in the history of Empire—with a
potential usurper, Mir Jaffir, a relation by marriage of the
Nawab's predecessor, Alivardi Khan.

On June 13, 1757, with the promise of Mir Jaffir's help,
Clive set out by land and water with 3,000 men to defeat
Nawab Siraj-ud-daula's 50,000. Of Clive's force, 250 were
from the 39th under Coote and Grant—now both majors—
and that admirable letter-writer, Captain Corneille.* Five
days later, as Coote and his men were taking the granaries
and fort at Cutwa, the monsoon burst over their heads, an
event which caused Clive some misgivings but which
contributed, incidentally, to the Nawab's downfall.

Of the Council of War on the 21st, Corneille says that a
great majority considered they were not strong enough to
go ahead. 'But on more maturely considering our situation,
that the longer we deferred attacking the Nawab the
stronger he would grow, that our delay might perhaps give
the French time to join him, that the danger of retreat
were greater than that of advancing . . . our proceeding was
resolved on by the Colonel . . .' Coote, that fire-eater, was
eloquently in favour, fearing among other things 'that
delay might cast a damp' on spirits roused by success.

It was a classic dilemma between caution and audacity;
but the risks were formidable. Clive thought about it for
an hour, and decided to proceed. In the afternoon of June 22
the little army set out to wade through the 15 miles of floods
between them and the Nawab, who was in an entrenched
camp on the Bograti River, north of the village of Plassey.
That night, soaking and exhausted, Clive made his dis-
positions in and around a mango orchard—to learn from

* His *Journal of my Service in India* (Folio Society 1966)—a
long letter to his father—is delightful; observant, objective and
entertaining.

Lt-General Sir Eyre Coote (1726–1783). Coote, one of the founders of British India, joined the 39th as a Captain in 1755 and fought at Plassey.

Mir Jaffir that the Nawab was on the move against them.

'Altogether', says Corneille, 'we were in such a situation as would have made us an easy prey to 400 men of any spirit that dared to have attacked us. But the enemy we had to encounter was luckily not of that stamp.'

That night they lay to their arms; and at sunrise next

morning, June 23, 1757, the Nawab advanced, 'affording us', Corneille says, 'a grand, though terrible, prospect'. He was not exaggerating. 35,000 infantry, 18,000 horsemen, 50 pieces of cannon mounted on great limbers towed by yokes of white oxen and with an elephant in attendance on each were heading their way, while '40 vagabond Frenchmen' set up four light cannon beside one of the dewponds and opened fire.

Clive was waiting for them in front of the orchard; but when the Nawab's artillery also opened up and casualties began to mount, he pulled his infantry back into the shelter of the trees, leaving his few light guns to fight it out with the Nawab's artillery as best they might. About noon it started to rain, and this, as it turned out was providential. The Nawab's gunners started to have trouble with damp powder, and their fire slackened and finally stopped altogether; Clive's artillery, however, 'which was very well served that day', kept firing and eventually succeeded in picking off the Nawab's best general, Mir Mudan.

To the wretched Siraj-ud-daula, surrounded by traitors and sycophants, this was a body-blow, and he ordered a general retreat into his camp. Immediately, and without orders, Clive's 2nd-in-command, Major Kilpatrick,* advanced with the 39th's Grenadiers. Clive was furious; but then, quickly summing up the situation, sent Coote and his company after them, and the foremost enemy positions were captured by the 39th. A further vigorous attack by Coote and the 39th's Grenadiers captured the remaining enemy positions. Though the '40 vagabond Frenchmen' kept up an effective fire and succeeded for a time in rallying the Nawab's fleeing troops, Clive's fieldpieces broke up the cavalry counter-attack, and ranged on the Nawab's camp; whereupon M. de St. Frais and his men realised that the day was lost and retired, without their

* An E I Company officer.

guns. In the meantime, Mir Jaffir detached his troops and, after some misunderstanding, joined Clive's forces.

And now the whole great bellowing mob of men and horses, camels and elephants and oxen, was in rout; by five that evening the camp with its hoard of booty was in Clive's hands, while Coote pursued the fleeing army for a further 6 miles on foot. The Battle of Plassey, which turned the English in India from a mercantile to a colonial role, and secured for the 39th a unique battle honour,* had been won—at a cost of 18 killed and 45 wounded, 4 of the latter being of the 39th.

The more palpable consequences of victory and defeat

---

* Plassey, and the motto 'Primus in Indis'. The latter survives in the cap and collar badges of the Devon and Dorset Regiment.

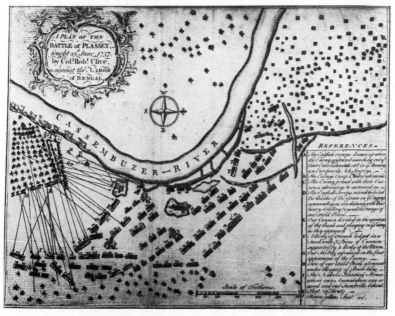

An early plan of the battle of Plassey, June 23, 1757. The British positions are in the mango orchard on the left.

are perhaps worth a mention. Clive received £234,000; the members of the Bengal Council between £10,000 and £80,000 each; the Army and Navy, £400,000 to be shared proportionately between them. The Nawab, Siraj-ud-daula, who had fled the field and halted at Murshidabad only long enough to pick up 'what money and jewels he could conveniently carry off, his favourite woman and a very small number of attendants', was identified, caught and killed within a fortnight. He was twenty.

Of the rest of the 39th's first tour in India there is little to be said. The unstoppable Coote chased the French out of Bengal in a three-month campaign which included floods, mutiny, fever and the loss of all the arrack; and Adlercron, with the rest of the Regiment in Madras, carried out a leisurely and ineffective sortie against them at Wandewash. It is legitimate to wonder whether the course of British history in India might not have run a rather different course if John Adlercron had succeeded in standing up for his rights and commanded at Plassey.

Before the end of 1757 the 39th were ordered back to England; but a good many officers and nearly all the men transferred to the Bengal European Regiment and to the Company's service in Madras. Of the officers, the most notable was Major Forde, who later defeated both the French and the Dutch; and a mere remnant mustered for the 11-month voyage home. Of these, one party was shipwrecked on the Irish coast and were set upon by wreckers who desisted, however, on coming whisker to whisker with their intended victims' mascot—a Bengal tiger cub.

Three years before this, in December 1755, 'Letters of Service' had been issued for the raising of ten new regiments. One of these, the 54th, was eventually to become the 2nd Battalion, the Dorsetshire Regiment.

Chapter

3

The 54th: 1755-1791

THE spur that rowelled the country into raising ten new regiments that year was a series of clashes in North America between the English colonists and the French. The 54th itself was raised by Lieutenant-Colonel John Campbell—eldest son of an earlier colonel of the 39th—at Salisbury, in the early months of 1756, though the 'Letters of Service' authorising the Regiment were dated December 23, 1755. Among its 750 men were 50 Highlanders, mustered by Campbell's Scottish connections, and a seasoning of veterans from other regiments, notably the 11th and the 36th. The facings to their scarlet tunics were 'popinjay green'—an unsatisfactory colour which was later changed to just green—and within four months they were ordered to Gibraltar. This did not at all suit the pressed men among them, who were brought to the borders of mutiny. In fact the 54th departed for its first service abroad disarmed and under guard.

They had hardly been on the Rock a month before they were caught for sea duty, just as the 39th had been forty years before. They saw little action with the squadron of Admiral John Byng—who was only a year away from execution for 'negligence' over the loss of Minorca—but suffered vilely from 'a ship's distemper'. Back in Gibraltar, Campbell transferred to the 14th Hussars (dying, a Field-Marshal, in 1806); and the Regiment kicked its heels until, in 1763, came peace, reduction, and transfer to Ireland.

It was a quiet time, and their Seven Years War arms gradually wore out in that gently corruptive climate, to be replaced just in time before they were ordered to America in 1775. There, in the wake of a succession of hamfisted attempts by George III and Lord North to bring the independently-minded colonists to heel, the port of Boston had been closed to British ships, and the first shots had been fired, at Concord, in April. But it was not for over a year, after a rough, two-month Atlantic crossing, that the 54th were in action.

Their first taste of the temper of the 'ten thousand peasants', as Burgoyne described the rebels, was unpromising, not to say ominous. In an ill-co-ordinated attempt upon Charleston with Commodore Parker's squadron in June, they were faced with a channel, The Breach, between the islands that guarded it that was too deep for wading and too shoal for boats, and with the rebel forces very ready to make the most of their predicament. The ships took a beating from the guns of Fort Sullivan; and the expedition was called off.

In August the Regiment landed at New York, and, as part of Major-General Pigot's 5th Brigade, was stationed on Staten Island. Here, though they missed most of the action, they had a series of quick successes. Commanded by General William Howe, the younger brother of Admiral Earl Howe, who was C-in-C, North America at the same time, the British Army defeated Sullivan at Flatbush, cleared Long Island, captured New York, and took Fort Washington at the northern end of Manhattan Island, overlooking the Hudson River.

This was the third successive defeat of Washington's forces in three months; but while Cornwallis set off in pursuit of the rebels across New Jersey, the 54th were sent north to occupy Rhode Island, which they did without loss, early in 1777. And there, for the next two years, they remained, and so missed the subsequent battles at Brandywine, Germantown and Monmouth Court House.

However, in February 1778 the French, encouraged by Burgoyne's surrender at Saratoga, entered the war on the colonists' side; and Sullivan, with the somewhat limp support of D'Estaing's squadron, made an attempt on Newport, but was smartly evicted from the island. Eighteen months later, to Admiral Rodney's disgust, Rhode Island was evacuated, and the 54th returned to New York. The following summer, in a devastating outbreak of typhus, they lost 30 men.

Apart from that, there is little to recount on the New York front at that time until, in September 1780, the calm was rudely shattered by the curious and unhappy affair of Major John André* and Benedict Arnold. André—gay, talented, ambitious and a charmer—is accorded a special niche in the history of the 54th, but he was only nominally a member of the Regiment. He had transferred into it from the 26th in order to remain in America, where he was ADC first to General Sir Charles ('No Flints') Grey, then to Grey's successor, Clinton, and at the time of his death was Deputy Adjutant General of the Army in America.

What happened was as follows. The American General, Benedict Arnold, smarting under injustices real and imagined, decided to defect to the British: his terms, £20,000 and a Major-Generalship in the British Army in exchange for the fortress at West Point. Clinton, through Arnold's agents Stansbury and Odell, accepted the deal in principle, and arranged for André to go and meet Arnold and settle the final details.

André, in uniform, duly proceeded up the Hudson in HMS *Vulture*, was picked up by rowing-boat, and met Arnold at the rendezvous on the river bank. Their business took them most of the night; and when André was ready to leave, it was discovered that *Vulture* had dropped downstream to avoid the gunfire of the American fort at Teller's Point. The boatman, who declined to make the trip in

---

* There is a Captain John André in the Regiment today, who is a descendant.

daylight, refused also to make it that evening; and Arnold suggested that, instead, André should put on civilian clothes and ride back to the British lines, and supplied him with a pass. It was a no-man's-land of woods and tracks, and André was nearly home when he was stopped by three rebel 'Skinners'—a cross between footpads and guerillas whose interest, ironically, was primarily in loot, not espionage.

They stripped him; and it was only when they found Arnold's papers with details of West Point, hidden in his boot, that they decided to hand him over to the American authorities. Arnold's safe conduct for 'Mr. Anderson' had already proved itself of doubtful value; it was a positive liability after Arnold, hearing of André's capture and his own incrimination, had made a dash for the *Vulture*, which was still waiting patiently for André. On board, and in New York, he received, not the acclaim he was expecting, but that morbid fascination tainted with revulsion which has always been the traitor's dubious homage.

Meanwhile, André himself was tried as a spy. He maintained that he was a prisoner-of-war; Clinton that the two had met on neutral ground under a flag of truce. The Court accepted neither view. 'Major André', they said, 'who came within our lines in the night on an interview with Major-General Arnold in an assumed character and was taken within our lines in a disguise with the enclosed papers concealed upon his person . . . ought to be considered a spy from the enemy, and . . . agreeable to the law and usage of nations, it is their opinion that he ought to suffer death'.

And death meant hanging. André's request that he should be shot 'like a gentleman' was rejected by Washington; so hanged he was, at Tappan, on October 2, 1780, in full regimentals, being, as he said, 'reconciled to my fate, but not to the mode'.

Arnold was made a Colonel, with the provisional rank

The 'spy', Major John André (1751–1780)—a self-portrait.

of Brigadier, was given some light employment—he was still suffering from wounds acquired at Saratoga—and was at Fort Griswold in Connecticut when the 54th stormed the ditch and only got over the palisade beyond by clambering on each other's backs. The fort had been reported easy game: the opposite was the truth; and it took threequarters of an hour of the warmest work to force back the picquets and subdue the garrison, and cost the Regiment 15 killed and 78 wounded. Subsequently New London fell and was burnt to the ground, its fate bestowing on the 54th the sobriquet of 'The Flamers'.

It was the 54th's last action of the war. Its Light Company

was already in enemy hands, having been with Cornwallis at the surrender at Yorktown in October 1781. Now the remainder were stationed in New York while peace was arranged in Paris; and in November 1783, when New York was finally evacuated by the British, were transferred to Nova Scotia.

For the next eight years they had an uneventful time in the Maritime Provinces, and the period would require only the briefest mention were it not for two members of the Regiment: Sergeant-Major William Cobbett and Major Lord Edward Fitzgerald. They make an intriguing contrast.

Fitzgerald, almost another John André for looks, charm and high spirits, joined the Regiment in New Brunswick in 1788—as a result, it is said, of unrequited love—though he had already fought with distinction in the American War in the 19th Foot. Like Sturt of the 39th in Australia forty years later, Fitzgerald was a born explorer, and made two notable journeys through the Canadian backwoods, where he met the Indians and was adopted by the Bear Tribe of the Hurons, and rounded off his second trip by descending the Mississippi to New Orleans. A year later, as a member of the Irish Parliament, he was dismissed the Army for supporting a toast at a banquet demanding 'the abolition of all hereditary titles and feudal distinctions'. After identifying himself with those who were working for an Irish Republic, he was finally betrayed in Dublin and shot while being arrested. He died from his wounds in Newgate gaol at the age of 35—an early, but by no means the last, martyr to the cause of Irish independence.

Cobbett, a Surrey smallholder's son, was born in the same year as Fitzgerald, and was in New Brunswick at the same time. It is improbable that they ever exchanged ideas; yet the Irish peer and the farmer's boy who was later to become the champion of rural England, might have found that they had quite a lot in common. Cobbett rose swiftly from corporal to RSM; but got his discharge when the Regiment came home, and promptly demanded the court-martial of three of his late officers on seventeen charges of making false musters and false clothing returns, and other peculations.

The officers were brought to trial; but Cobbett himself failed to appear, because, he complained, he had been unable to get the witnesses or the Regimental books he needed to support his accusations; and they were honourably acquitted. Since the offences Cobbett had charged them with were rife in the army of the eighteenth century, there was probably some truth in his accusations: but absconding was hardly the way to make them stick.

Chapter
4

The 39th: 1757–1803

WE left the 39th—'Adlercron's' until his death, as a
Lieutenant-General, in 1766—in Ireland, and
much reduced since their return from India.
There is little to report of them there; but in 1768 they were
brought up to establishment with Irish recruits, and sailed
for Gibraltar the following summer. At first there was
nothing to try them, beyond 'the same dull round', as one
officer put it, of garrison duty; though it is worth noting
that in 1770 they were instructed to form a Light Company
of intelligent and active men to act as skirmishers. This was
the fruit of Canadian experience during the Seven Years
War, when the limitations of the rigid infantry formation
had been clearly demonstrated.

The outbreak of the American War of Independence did
not much affect the Gibraltar garrison until Burgoyne's
defeat at Saratoga encouraged the French to make common
cause with the rebels, and the Spanish to try, once again, to
recover the Rock. The new siege began in the summer of
1779—the 54th were back in New York at that time, after
their spell in Rhode Island—with a close blockade; but it
was not until September that the garrison began to stir
things up by opening up on the besiegers in order to
disrupt their siege works. It is some index of the leisure-
liness of eighteenth century siege warfare that it was
exactly *four months* before their fire was returned.

1780 was marked by short rations, the inevitable scurvy
—which one cargo of lemons from Malaga was enough to
halt—lack of shoe leather, and the gradual advance of the
Spanish lines across the isthmus. The first real test came

Detail from a contemporary print in the Regimental Museum of the night sortie, November 27–28, 1781, against the Spanish lines during the Great Siege of Gibraltar.

in the spring of the following year, when the arrival of a large convoy provoked the Spaniards into a punishing bombardment, one of the side effects of which was to expose, all too literally, the hoarded wine-stocks of the local merchants—an early form of war-profiteering. The troops profited in turn, and it is recorded that 'their discipline was overpowered by their inebriation'.

The town was in ruins, but there was no assault. Life

for the besieged went on, rather like Londoners' during the Blitz; but in November they retaliated by creeping out at night in 'the greatest silence and regularity and [for once, presumably!] with no man in liquor'. The 39th led the centre column; they took the Spaniards by surprise, and in an hour of brilliantly organised destruction put 10 mortars and 18 guns out of action, blew up the main magazine, lit fires that burnt for a week, and undid months of painstaking work.*

Siege and resistance continued through 1782. In June, 4,000 Frenchmen joined the besiegers; and three months later they began a massive bombardment, both from their rebuilt lines and from floating batteries. Red-hot shot disposed of the latter; and although both did much damage, the actual achievement was nil. The Rock was continuously and closely invested now by French and Spanish fleets; nevertheless, in October, Howe slipped a large convoy in, and this gave the garrison the stores and reinforcements they needed to hold out for the remaining four months of the siege. By March 1783 it was all over. The names of two officers of the Regiment deserve a mention: Robert Boyd, the Colonel, who was Deputy Governor; and Captain J. Horsburgh, appointed Town Major, who wrote a lively account of the siege in his letters home.

General Elliott, the endlessly resourceful Governor, was awarded a well-deserved KCB; and the 39th, which had lost 2 officers and 65 men killed, got its second battle honour —the right to bear 'Gibraltar', 'Montis Insignia Calpe',† and the Castle and Key, on the Regimental Colour and Appointments. Once more the Rock had withstood the worst that those who coveted it could do; and at the end of 1783 the Regiment returned home.

* The 39th's part in the assault is commemorated in a vast mural in the patio of Government House, Gibraltar.
† The classical name for Gibraltar. With Abyla, across the Straits, it formed the Pillars of Hercules.

During their absence abroad, territorial titles had been introduced, and the 39th became associated with East Middlesex; but the connection was hypothetical, since there was no depot, and no link with the Militia. It was 1807 before they became associated with the county of Dorset, and 1879 before the Depot was established at Dorchester.

Meanwhile they had nearly ten years at home, covering the length and breadth of the British Isles from Mussel-burgh to the Isle of Man and from Galway to Southampton. Regularly they were inspected and reported on. In 1785, for instance, it is heartening to know that the officers were 'a genteel corps: very attentive and knew their duty'; less so, that the NCOs were 'not good in general', but the men were 'a good body, as times are'. Even in 1785, it seems, things weren't what they used to be.

In 1792, with a Republic, a revolutionary government,

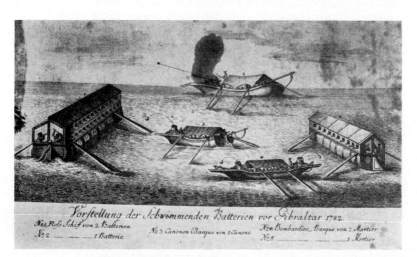

Floating batteries used in the massive attack on the Rock in June, 1782. According to the German caption they include 'Floss Schiff', 'Canonen Barque' and 'Bombardier Barque' armed with 'Batterien', 'Canone' and 'Mortier'.

and the Terror in full swing across the Channel, and the reformed armies on the loose in the Netherlands, we were at war once again with France; in the following year the 39th were sent to Barbados in pursuance of Pitt's strategy of striking at the French sugar islands in the Antilles. In February 1794, as part of a force that included the 15th, the 43rd, the 3rd Grenadiers and the 3rd LI,* under the command of General Sir Charles Grey, they landed at Martinique. Within a week much of the island was in their hands; within three, after the stirring rout of the mulatto Bellegarde, Fort Bourbon capitulated, and with it the island. Like all campaigns in those densely forested and rain-drenched islands, it was tough going while it lasted; and it was not long before their notorious climate began to thin the ranks.

From Martinique Grey went on to St. Lucia, which he subdued in a fortnight, and thence to Guadeloupe. Early successes, however, dissolved in the face of strong French reinforcements—Howe had still to assert British naval superiority on 'the Glorious First of June'—and the inevitable fever. A brisk victory by the 39th at Point St. Jean was followed by their being trapped in Berville Camp, near the isthmus that joins Basse Terre and Grande Terre. They held out for a week against vastly superior numbers, in one attack inflicting 700 casualities for the loss of 20 of their own men, but, beyond help, were finally forced to surrender. Though the Colours were saved by Captains Parry and Bell, who escaped with them to one of the British islands in an open boat, the 39th was virtually wiped out. The survivors were drafted into other regiments; and the few remaining officers and NCOs returned to England to try and re-raise the Regiment.

The situation in the West Indies after the failure at Guadeloupe was full of menace. French propaganda and

* East Yorkshire Regt., 1st Oxfordshire and Buckinghamshire LI (Royal Green Jackets) and the Buffs.

French revolutionary sentiments were setting the slaves alight; and while the 54th were sent to secure St. Vincent, the re-formed 39th, after a terrible and abortive two-month passage to St. Domingo in which they lost 40 dead, without ever reaching their destination—a grim glimpse of what trooping could be like in the days of sail—ended up on the north-east coast of South America, and spent the next six years in Demerara and Surinam.

There, during the hurricane season, it was nothing exceptional to lose 30 men a month; and when in 1803, after seven years in the West Indies, the Regiment landed at Portsmouth from the *Thalia*, they were down to 17 officers and 365 men, of whom 50 were ill. And this despite having had their numbers kept up by 'culprits'—in other words, criminals.

During the Regiment's time abroad, war against revolutionary France had waxed, lapsed into the brief truce of Amiens, and flared up once more. Now, not only had they to try and make up their numbers in a seller's market, but were called upon to raise a second battalion. The first operation took six months: the second, with the splendid Hon. Robert O'Callaghan as Lieutenant-Colonel, was up to strength in three. Both battalions were to be usefully employed during the next dozen years; but there, for the moment, we must leave them, and pick up the 54th, recently returned from Canada, and recovering from the high-minded accusations of ex-Sergeant-Major William Cobbett.

Chapter
5

The 54th: 1791–1810

THE 54th did not stay long at home. In 1793 they were sent to reinforce the garrison on Guernsey; six months later, expecting to join Grey's West Indian force, like the 39th, they were diverted to Ostend instead, where the Duke of York was in trouble. Altogether between 1793 and 1795 the Regiment was sent to, or withdrawn from, the continent no less than four times, including a totally abortive expedition to Brittany, and at one stage spent an unimaginable four months cooped up in transports while Pitt and his ministers tried to decide what to do with them. Their final winter in the Netherlands was a miserable series of halts and retreats in vile weather. It was a campaign, notes the Regimental historian, which 'makes painful reading, not because our troops ever failed in battle but because so much suffering and loss were incurred to so little purpose'.

Emaciated, they returned home in the May of 1795, only to be packed off two months later to St. Vincent in the West Indies. The French, still in the ascendant, were busy encouraging the dissidents in every British-held island, including the fanatically courageous Caribs; and in a couple of hard-fought engagements the 54th had no chance to distinguish themselves and suffered severely. The climate as usual, winnowed the survivors; those who were still on their feet were drafted to the 63rd, while the officers and NCOs returned home to raise a new Regiment. It had happened to the 39th; to a greater or lesser degree it happened to every regiment that served in the West Indies in the eighteenth century.

In the meantime, in Ireland, rebellion was in the wind; and the Regiment, still a mere shadow, was despatched to King's County. They were there when Fitzgerald was caught; but were involved neither with that, nor with the defeat of the rebels at Vinegar Hill, though they marched to head off the 1,200 French who landed in Killala Bay in August 1798. They were not engaged; and indeed saw little of all the desperate misery and cruelty that marked the 'troubles' of '98.

It is one of the persistent ironies of the history of Britain, and of the British Army, that Ireland, which provided regular employment for British regiments over two and a half centuries, provided also a great proportion of the rank and file in those very regiments. Thus the 54th, which landed in Ireland in 1798 a mere 150 strong, left two years later with over 1,200, and were split into two battalions. But they still had one more fiasco to endure—the ill-conceived attempts on the Spanish arsenals at Ferrol and Cadiz in August 1800—before their first chance of glory. This was to be in Egypt, where Napoleon's vaunted *Armée de l'Orient* had been cut off by Nelson's victory of the Nile, and was ripe for expulsion.

General Abercromby prepared the expedition with great care. Spells ashore in Minorca and Malta got the troops fit; and assault training at Marmorice in Turkey brought them to battle pitch. Then, early on March 8, 1801, after a frustrating week's delay offshore because of weather, the force, which included among its 17,000 the whole of the 1st, and 200 of the 2nd Battalion, squeezed into the boats and began the long row into Aboukir Bay.

They came under fire almost immediately, had a harrowing passage, and were attacked the moment the boats grounded. However, every attempt by the French to drive them back into the sea was repulsed; and by evening, at a cost of 750 casualties, they were firmly established ashore. With 5 killed and 19 wounded, the 54th had got off lightly.

Five days later Abercromby advanced along the sandy spit between Lake Mareotis and the sea towards Alexandria. But at the end of a hard day's slog, during which the Regiment had been subjected to 'an exterminating fire' by the French artillery, they had been stopped in their tracks. A week later the French counter-attacked. This proved to be a very tough battle. Abercromby himself was mortally wounded and British losses were 1,500; but it was the crisis of the expedition, and a salutary lesson for Menou's veterans of the Italian campaign, who had deemed themselves invincible. So discomfited were they that they retired behind their fortifications, and the initiative returned firmly and finally into British hands. General Hutchinson, Abercromby's successor, marched on Cairo, while Major-General Coote (a nephew of Eyre Coote's) kept Menou bottled up in Alexandria.

As soon as reinforcements arrived Coote launched a cunningly planned assault on the city. The 1/54th's objective was Fort Marabout, which stood guard over the old harbour. By dragging up two batteries of guns—hot, dry work over rocks and sand—under the accurate covering fire of the Light Company's sharpshooters, they succeeded in isolating the fort and silencing its fire. Before the final, full-scale assault was launched, the Commandant surrendered.

The fall of Fort Marabout—for which, forty years later, the 54th were awarded a unique battle honour—was the key that opened the gate of Alexandria. Coote was able to fight his way to the outer defences protected by the flanking fire of gunboats in the old harbour; and on August 26 Menou asked for terms.

The six-months campaign in Egypt is significant for being the first substantial success against the rampaging armies of revolutionary France; and it thereby 'revived confidence and an honourable pride in the military service'—which was more than could be said for the strategy of the preceding eight years. But the victory had not been cheap.

The Marabout Gun, a souvenir of the capture of the fort by the 54th in August 1801, which accompanied the Regiment on its travels for 40 years, and is now in the Museum. The gun, a six-pounder, is original: the carriage dates from 1828.

Apart from the high action casualties, fever and dysentery were prevalent, and acute ophthalmia robbed hundreds of men permanently of their sight.

In October 1801 peace was patched up between the combatants, and two months later the 54th returned to Gibraltar. There the 2nd Battalion was disbanded; while the 1st was called upon to suppress a Christmas Eve mutiny, provoked by the Duke of Kent's tightening up of discipline and closing down of some of the town's more pernicious drink-shops. The counter-attraction of wet canteens, selling something a little less corrosive than the local fire-water, failed to appease one or two of the rowdier battalions, who went berserk and swarmed through the town. The 54th, 90 per cent of whom were Irish, rejected an invitation from the drunks to join them, and dispersed them with one sharp volley instead. Their 'steady discipline and good conduct' was attributed to their CO, Colonel Ross, who was promoted on the strength of it, and earned them a silver punch-bowl from the Duke of Kent, whose life they had safeguarded. Thus was started a link between the Regiment and the Royal House of Kent which was revived when HRH Princess Marina became Colonel-in-Chief in 1953.

Though impervious to the bacillus of mutiny, they succumbed to the 'inflammatory fever' which swept through the garrison in 1804, and lost a hundred men in four months. One of its more embarrassing side-effects was that the sufferers' hair fell out; and while on the subject of hair, it was during these years that the pigtail, dressed with tallow, was finally abolished in the British Army.

In 1805 the Regiment returned to England. One transport, however, fell foul of a French Squadron off Brest and was captured. Their wanderings over the next two years comprise a bizarre little story in themselves, and are part of a larger episode no less bizarre.

The prisoners—men of the 54th and the Queen's— were put aboard the frigate *Volontaire*, which herself fell foul of two British cruisers. She took to her heels and was pursued southwards, eventually arriving at the Cape of Good Hope, which, as it happened, we had just captured from the Dutch. Unaware of the colony's change of ownership, the *Volontaire*'s captain sailed cheerfully into Table Bay—and straight under the guns of a British 64. He had no alternative but to surrender; and the 54th, free men once more, promptly found themselves involved in another wild adventure.

Commodore Home Popham—a forbear of the present writer, and a sailor of vigorous, if erratic, energies—had become taken with the notion of furthering the war-effort by capturing Buenos Ayres from the Spanish; and this, in

July 1806, and with part of the Cape garrison, he proceeded to do. However, he was not strong enough to hold it; and when reinforcements—among them 110 men of the 54th—arrived in October, they found that the original expedition had themselves been captured, but Popham, still bubbling with optimism, was anchored off Maldonado, eighty miles from Monte Video, and all set to continue his private war.

He now had support from the Ministry of All the Talents at home; and while further reinforcements were on the way, the 54th took to horseback and had some somewhat chastening brushes with the more nimble local horsemen. When reinforcements, under Lieutenant-General Sir Samuel Auchmuty arrived, the force attacked and captured Monte Video in the face of stiff opposition and for the price of 500 casualties; but failed to retake Buenos Ayres. Whereupon the Commodore's South American brainwave fizzled ignominiously out.

In the meantime the remainder of the Regiment had been ordered to Jamaica. As usual, a combination of yellow jack and cheap rum did their deadly work; and there was some restlessness, and an insignificant mutiny, among the negro soldiers of the 2nd West India Regiment. The monotony was interrupted in 1809 when, in response to a call for help against the French by the Spaniards in Santo Domingo, Major-General Carmichael led a small expedition there, and swiftly captured the city and the neighbouring Fort Jerome.

The 54th began to trickle home from Jamaica in the same year, but it was 1813 before the last contingent arrived. By then recruiting—again, mostly of Irishmen—had brought its numbers up to around 600, and it was ready for another of those odd, inconclusive little campaigns which were becoming something of a speciality of the 54th's.

Chapter
6

The 39th: 1803–1814

WE left the 39th in the year 1803 on their return to England from Surinam, having just successfully raised a 2nd Battalion, the Colonel of which was one of the Regiment's most bracing characters, Robert O'Callaghan, ex-Light Dragoons. For the first two years both battalions remained stationed in south-east England, while Bonaparte built up his invasion forces in Boulogne, stared across the Straits through a spy-glass, and nerved himself for the crossing.

By 1805, although invasion was still a theoretical possibility, a new coalition, which included Austria and Russia, was being formed, the Army was vastly increased, and Pitt had some scope to plan a new strategy. As so often, the Mediterranean was of prime concern. The French were back in Naples, and might well move into Sicily; and so in March the 1/39th left England for Malta. Their passage south coincided with Villeneuve's escape from Toulon— the start of the chase that was to end six months later at Trafalgar—and they were delayed in the Tagus, and again at Gibraltar, until the coast was clear. As a result they did not reach Malta until mid-July, and Sicily for four months after that.

There some of them remained for nearly five years, while the threat of a French invasion of the island came and went. Murat made one attempt—repulsed with heavy losses—in which the 39th were not involved: their occupation, uneventful though it was, comprises an odd and little-known incident in the Regiment's history, though one that was to be repeated, with variations, 140 years later.

In August 1811 they received their orders to move to
Cadiz, and so to the Peninsula, where the 2nd Battalion
had already been kept busy for the previous two years.

Since 1809 and Wellesley's first success against the
French at Talavera, the initiative in Spain had gradually
but steadily shifted to the British and their allies. A combination of Wellington's scorched earth policy, and the
impregnable defence lines of Torres Vedras forced Massena
to retreat in the spring of 1811; but the 2nd Battalion saw
little action until Albuhera, in May of that year. They were
commanded by Patrick Lindsay, of the 78th Highlanders,
who was to stay with the Regiment until 1837, when he was
promoted to Major-General, and is one of its sturdiest
characters. As sturdy, but more picturesque, was the
extraordinary Irishman, Captain Bryan Burrough O'Toole,
who had fought with the Irish, the French, the Austrians
and the Prussians—and even survived a dreadful campaign
in Santo Domingo—before joining the 39th in 1803. This
wild soldier of fortune remained with the Regiment until
1813, when he commanded a Portuguese brigade; he is
reputed to have fought in more campaigns than any other
soldier of his time.

At Albuhera, Soult attempted to turn the right flank of
the British force on the undulating ground south of the
village. The French attack was already blunted when the
battalion, as part of Abercrombie's brigade, hurled themselves upon 'the frowning masses' of the French Grenadiers
and steadily drove them back, while the 4th Division smashed
the point of the hook, Latour-Maubourg's cavalry.

For all that Wellington, who was not himself in command,
called it 'a strange concern', and it was undoubtedly an
expensive victory, Albuhera is famous in the annals of the
British infantry for the steadiness and valour with which
they outfaced an immensely powerful attack; and it seems
to have been one of those battles which have a tonic effect
on the victors, and very much the opposite on the losers.

'The memory of it', writes Sir Arthur Bryant, 'haunted them thereafter in the presence of the British infantry like a blow across the eyes'. Although the 2/39th escaped more lightly than some, they suffered a 20 per cent casualty rate—the third highest—and they justly bear the name of Albuhera on their Colours.

If that was something of a classic infantry battle their next was something of a tour de force. General Hill,* hearing that Girard's Division was out of touch with the main French forces on a foraging expedition—supplies were a constant anxiety to the French, since they aimed to live off the country—made a series of tremendous forced marches over the mountains in vile weather to catch the Frenchmen napping at Arroyo dos Molinos. Surprise was so complete that the first they knew of an attack was the sound of the pipers of the 92nd; the trap so well laid and so neatly sprung that they found themselves pinned against the Sierra de Montanches with every exit blocked. Those who escaped did so by mountaineering; and the 2nd Division, exhausted, soaked, hungry and nearly barefoot, had to let them go. But it was a worthwhile victory, 'the severest service we have had in the Peninsula', said one, and satisfactorily rounded off the 2nd Battalion's service there. Now, at the end of 1811, and less 380 men transferred to the 1st Battalion, the 2nd left Spain, and were back in England by the following spring.

The 2nd Division, to which the 1/39th were attached, was nicknamed 'The Observing Division'; and indeed, for almost a year, it was outside the action, marching many weary miles—including much of the long road to Madrid and back—suffering considerably in the process, but without the consolations of a scrap. And all the time Wellington with the main army was in the thick of it,

---

* 'Daddy' Hill was Wellington's most trusted subordinate. One of his descendants, Lieutenant-Colonel R. G. Hill, served in the Dorsets from 1933–58.

beating '40,000 Frenchmen in 40 minutes' at Salamanca in June of 1812, retaking Badajoz and Ciudad Rodrigo, and failing to take Burgos. The end of that year saw the Duke's last retreat in the Peninsula: orderly and measured, but miserable and hungry, on a diet of acorns and lean bullock.

Although, as Wellington had cautiously written eighteen months earlier '[the war] has become, to a certain degree, offensive on our part', and it could be stated categorically that the French could never now drive the British out as Soult had hoped to do four years before, there were still 200,000 of them in Spain at the beginning of 1813. Before the year was out there were, in effect, none. In that final expulsion, the 1/39th had a lively and important share.

The campaign started in May, the battalion, still part of Hill's Division (O'Callaghan now commanded the brigade), sweeping north-east, past Salamanca, past Burgos, hard on the heels of Joseph Bonaparte and Marshal Jourdain who finally turned to give battle at Vittoria. In this battle, the climax of a month's superb manoeuvering, and Wellington's finest accomplishment, the Division was on the British right, and steadily drove the French back along the foot of the Puebla hills; but it was no walkover. Wellington himself recorded that 'the contest here was . . . very severe, and the loss sustained considerable': they had a third of the French infantry facing them; resistance was tough, and the French counter-attacks formidable. However, by the time Wellington's attack in the centre had gained momentum, the French were already in retreat; and massed British artillery clinched the matter. Joseph and his army fled along the rough road to Pamplona, leaving behind them 150 guns, and the accumulated plunder of five years in Spain.

This last was too much for the troops. 'The soldiers', wrote Wellington to Bathurst, 'have got among them about a million sterling in money . . . the night of the battle, instead of being passed in getting rest and food to prepare

The battle of Vittoria, June 21, 1813, at which the 1/39th fought with distinction.

for the pursuit of the following day, was passed by the soldiers in looking for plunder . . . they were totally knocked up'.

All the same, within two weeks, these same soldiers were in the Pyrenean passes, and looking down on to the southern plains of France. But there was some hard fighting yet, and not so far ahead. On July 7 Wellington in person launched the attack on Gazan's forces holding the Pass of Maya. This was mountain fighting; and O'Callaghan's Brigade were working their way forward when fog came down, and they ran straight into French fire at close quarters. The next half hour or so were quite macabre, with the French, whose voices could be clearly heard, charging again and again through the mist, to be met by volley after volley at point-blank range and driven back. 'If the sea fog had held off for an hour or two longer',

Wellington wrote in his marvellous dry way, 'we should have made a good thing of it'.

As it was, Soult carried out a swift and drastic reorganisation of the French forces; and a fortnight later they attacked with the advantage both of numbers and surprise. In the resulting confusion the outstanding feature was the tenacity of the defence. The 39th, hurriedly rushed forward to help try and stem the assault, fought like tigers. When, at last, they were driven back, it was 'with the most deliberate pace' and with O'Callaghan 'amidst the din of arms calling to his soldiers with the voice of a stentor, "Steady, 39th; ordinary time!" '. The attack on the Pass of Maya cost the French 2,000 men before the 2nd Division retreated in good order to Elizondo, five miles in rear. The 39th's casualties were 10 officers and 175 men killed, wounded, captured or missing; and the battle stands high in the record of the 2nd Division, and of the Regiment.

It was the last French throw in Spain. Soult's one further attempt miscarried; and by the beginning of August the 1/39th were back on the Pass of Maya, after a weary week with 'no baggage, no blankets, marching day and night, nothing but our rations', as one disgruntled officer wrote, and one sharp action at Venta de Urroz.

There followed three months rest for the battalion until, in the autumn, with Santander and Pamplona secure behind him, Wellington continued his advance. The 2nd Division had little work at the crossing of the Nivelle in November; but St. Pierre, a month later, on December 13, proved one of the toughest battles of the whole campaign. In a last, desperate attempt by Soult to stem Wellington's advance near Bayonne, the 28th and the 39th—about 1,500 strong—succeeded in stopping about 5,000 of the 'parlez-vous', and even found an opportunity to support the threatened centre. It was stiff while it lasted; but it drove Soult back behind his entrenchments at Bayonne.

Two months later he abandoned the west coast altogether,

and beat a fighting retreat eastwards to Toulouse. There was one brief, vivid incident near the village of Garris, when 'Old Nosey' himself rode up and gave the order: 'That hill must be taken before dark!' It was obeyed to the letter, though the defenders were seasoned troops who came forward, says the Regimental historian, 'cheering and with drums beating the charge'. Three times it came to cold steel; and the mighty O'Callaghan, leading charge after charge, was obliged, at one point, to dispose of three simultaneous assailants with his sword. In half an hour victory—very much the 39th's show—was complete, and the French fled away in the thickening dark.

There were a few more engagements—Orthez, as far as the 39th were concerned, was one—and some street fighting in the outskirts of Toulouse, before Soult abandoned that city, and Napoleon his empire. It was April 1814, and the Peninsular War was over. Between them in five years' campaigning, the two battalions of the 39th had gained seven battle honours for the Colours: Peninsula, common to them both; Albuhera by the 2nd; Vittoria, Pyrenees, Nivelle, Nive and Orthez by the 1st.

War-weary and travel-stained as they were, the 1/39th were on the march once more, almost before the battle-smoke had blown clear of Toulouse, for Bordeaux and passage to Canada, where, in good time, we will pick them up. For the moment, however, we must go back four years, to 1810, and rejoin the 54th, which we left reforming after their return from Jamaica.

Chapter
7
The 54th: 1810–1840

IT WAS an odd coincidence that not long after the 39th had been off the normal British army maps, in Sicily, the 54th should have been sent to an equally unusual station, Stralsund, in Sweden, to lend support to Napoleon's renegade Count Bernadotte. This turned out to be garrison duty of an arduous, but relatively peaceful, kind; and although they did march out once at Bernadotte's request, they saw no action. After Napoleon's defeat at Leipzig in October 1813, they were no longer needed, and set sail for Yarmouth, en route for Spain.

However, with the situation in Europe suddenly in flux, they were diverted to the Netherlands. Through the bitter winter they had only one engagement to relieve the monotony—the short, sharp attack on Merxem, outside Antwerp. On Napoleon's abdication, they formed part of the occupation forces in the Netherlands; and they were still there when he escaped from Elba ten months later, and so were present at Waterloo in June. But not for the first or last time, the Regiment was out of luck, being posted on the extreme right, at Hal, as a reserve to cover the Channel ports, where they neither saw nor heard anything of the crucial battle being waged ten miles away. Thus they were awarded no battle honour; but, by way of compensation, they shared in the bounty afterwards: £433 for field officers; £90 for captains; £35 for subalterns; £19 for sergeants; and £2 10s. for private soldiers, and were awarded the Waterloo Medal and laurel wreath.

After four months in the Bois de Boulogne with the army of occupation, the 54th returned to England, to be immediately drafted on 'law and order' duty in Liverpool, where the end of the war had created the usual disruptions, exacerbated by a bad harvest. Apart from one company that garrisoned Heligoland for a time, the Regiment spent the next two years in England; and then, at the end of 1818, marched from Lancashire to Portsmouth—it took them a month—under sailing orders for South Africa.

This time, instead of being swept off on some hare-brained adventure in South America they were given the more prosaic duty of countering Kaffir raiding-parties on the colony's eastern border; and, as a result of their work, a kind of buffer-state was set up between blacks and whites; and the young settlement got some peace.

Frontier work in Cape Colony may have been primitive, but at least it was healthy. When the Regiment moved to India in 1822, their arrival at Madras coincided with a cholera epidemic which wiped out 60 men, including 5 sergeants, at a blow.

They also acquired another 'legend' in the shape of their new Lieutenant-Colonel, Colquhoun Grant of the 11th Foot, who had been Wellington's Head of Intelligence, and whose earlier exploits in the Peninsula had included capture at Salamanca, a dashing escape, and a trip to Paris in the guise of an American and the company of one of Napoleon's Generals.

The Regiment spent the next two years in Bangalore; and when, in 1824, the Burmese War broke out and they were ordered to Arakan in company with the 42nd and the 62nd Bengal Native Infantry, they were in excellent shape, thanks mainly to Grant's care and influence. In view of what lay ahead of them, it was just as well.

The main attack on Ava, up the Irrawaddy, though attended with every kind of hazard from monsoon floods to the 'King's Invincibles' with gold and precious stones set in their skin, was successful: the Arakan campaign, on the other hand, was a disaster. It started well enough, with the capture of Ramree Island and a slow but effective advance up the Arakan River. Several of the strongly built and held stockades were taken, and the city of Arakan itself occupied. The Burmese were well armed, with muskets, swords, spears and a considerable artillery, and they usually fought well until, faced with steadiness and determination, they broke and fled. It was not they, however, but the country and the rains that brought the expedition to a standstill in the latter half of 1825.

For all practical purposes, the range of mountains that separated them from Ava, the capital, was impassable; dysentery and fever did the rest; and when General Morrison pulled out at the end of the year, the Regiment had gained a battle honour, Ava, but had lost 344 officers and men. In Burma, as in India and the West Indies, and in the troopships that plied between, the rudimentary medicine and primitive hygiene of the time were totally inadequate to prevent or control the fearsome local diseases —malaria, blackwater and yellow fever, dysentery, cholera and the rest; and it was not until Florence Nightingale took matters in hand after the scandal of the Crimean War and laid down new standards of sanitation and habitation for the cantonments in India, and for military hospitals in general, that the appalling mortality rate among British soldiers began to fall. The figures for the 54th in India in the years immediately after the 1st Burma War give the picture: in 1828, 37 deaths; in 1829, 39; in 1830—a good year—22; in 1831, 28; with an average daily sick-list of between 50 and 100. Against the names of many of those who died the entry read: 'Worn out man . . . due to be discharged'. Those who are quick to decry Britain's imperial past tend to forget the price that was paid for it in life and health. In the case of the 54th, in addition to all those in the cantonment cemeteries, a further 200 died or were invalided within two years of the Regiment's return home.

The Indian years of the Regiment between 1826 and

General Sir Mildmay Fane (1797–1868): CO of the 54th from 1829–1851: Colonel of the Regiment 1860–1868.

1840 were largely uneventful; but one name must be put on record, that of Lieutenant-Colonel Mildmay Fane, a Peninsular veteran who joined the 54th from the 98th Foot in 1832, commanded it for twenty-two years, and was Colonel of the Regiment from 1860 until his death eight years later.

When, in 1840, the Regiment was ordered home and volunteers to remain in India were called for, no less than

250 stepped forward; so a mere 20 officers and 360 other ranks embarked on the East Indiamen for the five-month voyage to England at the end of March. In this context it is interesting to note that although the Suez Canal was still thirty years ahead, it was not uncommon for officers to travel up the Red Sea, then overland to Port Said, and resume their voyage home, thereby saving themselves months at sea.

Chapter
8

The 39th: 1814–1881

IN 1814 the 2/39th were in England, recruiting; and the 1st Battalion, having chased the French out of Spain, were called upon to chase the Americans out of Canada. It was an odd, amphibious war they now became engaged in, and 2 officers and 60 men were quickly seconded aboard Captain Downie's naval squadron on Lake Cham-

A bandsman of the 39th, 1816. (From a drawing by N. Finart in the Royal Collection. Reproduced by gracious permission of Her Majesty the Queen.)

plain. Plattsburg had been captured; and it was calculated that a naval victory on the lake would enable Prévost to clear the Americans out of Quebec.

Unfortunately, Downie, far from defeating his American opponents, was himself annihilated, and Prévost, who was on the verge of success, broke off the action and retired across the frontier. It was the 39th's sole, somewhat ignominious, taste of that somewhat ignominious little war; for Napoleon was at large once more, and every available regiment was being rushed back to Europe. The 39th were not the only ones to arrive too late for Waterloo; instead of a battle, they were let in for three years of occupation duty in north-eastern France.

If India supplies one of the unchanging strands in the history of the British Army in the nineteenth century, Ireland provides another—then, and before, and after. When the 39th did a tour there from 1818–22, the country was going through one of its periodic spells of 'troubles'; and detachments were kept busy protecting the excisemen in their thankless task of tracking down illicit stills, 'aiding the civil power', and generally attempting to keep the peace. And as usual, when they could not deal with the native Irish in any other way, they recruited them: in 1821 a third of the rank and file were Irish.

From suppressing Irish rebels the battalion was turned to guarding English convicts. Between 1825 and 1827 they left England in small parties for Botany Bay, each being in charge of a shipload of prisoners under sentence of transportation. The penal settlement had been started in 1787; and by nature of its remoteness, and the will to survive of those who were sent there, was beginning to grow into a regular colony. Inevitably there were wild men among them, organising themselves into gangs and operating a reign of terror.

The tracking down of these ruffians, as well as plain warders' work—for the convicted were still treated as

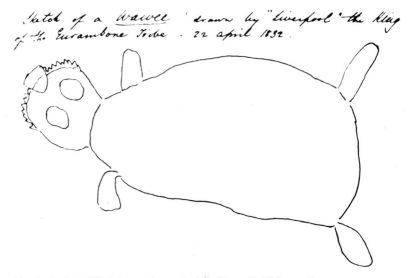

*Sketch of a duck-billed platypus by an aborigine king called 'Liverpool';
from Captain J. D. Forbes' New South Wales diary of 1832.*

criminals even in those inimical surroundings—fell to the
39th; and the names of Captains Walpole, Forbes, Wakefield,
Barker and Sturt, and Lieutenant Maule—all of the
Regiment—belong on any list of those who, in the course
of duty, helped to open up the Australian hinterland. Of
them all, Charles Sturt was perhaps the most enterprising:
his explorations resolved the then unknown course of the
Murray and Darling rivers, and he is regarded as the
founder of South Australia.* All these officers' journeys—
Sturt's second covered 2,000 miles, much of it, like
Stanley's in Central Africa sixty years later, by means of a
collapsible boat carried in sections—took him through
territory that was utterly unknown, largely waterless, and

* The centenary of his journey was commemorated by the issue
of two Australian stamps bearing his portrait, and the terse
legend: *Sturt-Explorer.*

not infrequently inhabited by hostile natives. Barker, in fact, lost his life to the latter in 1831.

In 1832 the battalion, having completed its statutory six years, left Australia for India, having, by the curiosity and adventurousness of its officers, left a permanent trace of its sojourn on the map of the continent.

And so, after an interval of seventy-five years, the Regiment which had been 'Primus in Indis'—the honours, of which they had been arbitrarily deprived by the Inspector of Colours in 1807 were returned to them in 1835—returned there. It was much changed since the days of Clive and 'John Company'. The factories had grown into provinces; a trading venture had become the civil power over much of the country.

The Regiment's first six years were spent in Bangalore. During that time they lost 300 men through death and invaliding; and the monotony of cantonment life was interrupted several times by the call for punitive expeditions. The first of them, in 1834, was directed against the Rajah of Coorg in Mysore, lasted three weeks, was entirely successful despite difficult country and some determined opposition, and is chiefly interesting as an example of the *ad hoc* nature of the British conquest of India. The Rajah's cruelty and excesses led to intervention by the Madras Government and the Army; intervention led to the Rajah's defeat and surrender, which, in turn, left a political vacuum that had to be filled. One souvenir of the campaign, the Rajah's bronze gong, became the guardroom time-signal, and has been used ever since.

Similar brisk campaigns were required in 1837 in Canara and Malabar, and in 1839 against the Nawab of Kurnool, who was also summarily deposed.

Rather more taxing was the expedition against the Mahrattas that followed in the wake of the 1st Afghan War—for which the 39th had been on call, though they had not been needed. Like the Afghan war itself, the

*Members of the 39th in Bengal, circa 1845, shortly after Maharajpore.
From a contemporary sketch by an unknown hand.*

Gwalior campaign was sparked off by the emergence of a
ruler offensive to the British Government. Despite con-
ciliatory noises, the Mahrattas were ready for a scrap, and
the British 'Army of Observation', to give it its euphemistic
title, 10,000 strong and commanded by the C-in-C, Sir
Hugh Gough, came up with them outside Maharajpore at
the end of 1843.

In the first phase of the battle, the 39th advanced,
without firing a shot, through a barrage of cannonballs,
grape, canister and old horseshoes, to capture thirty guns
at bayonet point: in the second, the main trouble came
from snipers concealed in, or behind, stooks of corn, and
these too were flushed out by bayonet: in the third and
final phase, the 39th's grenadiers took a ferociously defended
four-gun battery by a *coup de main*. For their distinguished
part in this sharp and bloody battle—for which their
casualties were 28 killed and 187 wounded, among them

Major Bray, the acting CO, and his Ensign son, who was killed while carrying the Queen's Colour*—the Regiment were awarded a battle honour, a special bronze star struck from the captured guns and six months' 'batta', i.e., supplementary allowance.

The following year the volunteering that always preceded a move back to England was invited, and more than 500 decided to stay on in India. It was in this manner that Sergeant Power and 16 men of the 13th LI had been transferred to the 39th when they made their famous assault on the Heights of Truckee in Baluchistan, after which the six who were killed were later found to have been awarded the Baluchi's highest token of courage—a red thread tied round each man's wrist—as a kind of posthumous VC given by the enemy. This incident, so typical of the extraordinary, almost casual valour of the British soldier of the last century, earned a stirring ballad from Sir F. H. Doyle, and links the 39th and the 13th more firmly than the mythical connection between 'Pearce's Dragoons' and 'Sankey's Horse'.

In 1847 the Regiment returned to England, after twenty-two years abroad. The next thirty-seven were to be peaceful ones, interrupted only by the Crimean War. The 39th had moved from Ireland to Gibraltar when it started, and were not transferred to the Black Sea until early in 1855. By February they had been brought forward to the siege-works in front of Sevastopol. That dilatory and desultory investment dragged on all summer, with snipers, illness and an occasional bombardment or Russian counter-attack to contend with. The action was largely elsewhere—at the Battle of Tchernaya in August, and the Malakoff in September, after which the Russians evacuated the city, and another Crimean winter—the last—closed in.

* Ensign Bray's tunic is in the Dorsets' Museum, and a descendant, Lieutenant-Colonel H. A. A. Bray, is still serving in the Regiment.

Officers of the 39th in the Crimea, 1855—one of Roger Fenton's famous photographs.

For this nugatory and uncomfortable service all ranks received a medal, and the Colours the addition of 'Sevastopol'; and the Regiment went off to Canada for three peaceful years, to Bermuda for five, for four less peaceful ones to an Ireland being stirred up by the Fenians, and, in 1869, back once more to India. This was all part of the Victorian military pattern, in which soldiers played the part of a world police-force.

They were not entirely static, though, those mid-years of Victoria's reign. Weapons were being steadily improved; and the muzzle-loading rifle, the introduction of which, with its greased cartridge-cap, in 1851, sparked off the Indian Mutiny six years later, was itself replaced by the breech-loading Snider in 1868. And in the same year, Edward Cardwell, Gladstone's Secretary of State for War, began his programme of major reform that was to change the Army more radically than at any time in its history. Commission purchase was abolished; short service introduced; and battalions were linked in pairs, one at home and one abroad. For the 39th, with only one battalion (the 2nd had been disbanded after the Napoleonic Wars) this meant a link with the 75th, once a Highland regiment. But this was an interim arrangement only. In 1881, in a further series of reforms—comparable in their impact and the opposition they stirred up to those of recent years— regiments lost their treasured numbers, and two single-battalion regiments were permanently connected under a county title. Thus the 39th—which had held the county title of Dorsetshire since 1807—and the 54th—similarly connected with West Norfolk—were merged to become the 1st and 2nd Battalions, the Dorsetshire Regiment, while the 75th became the 1st Gordon Highlanders.

Chapter

9

The 54th: 1840–1881

URING the decade from 1830–40, both the 39th and the 54th were in southern India, though they never met; and in the latter year, the 54th returned to England. There they suffered a blow to Regimental pride when the War Office decreed that the Marabout Gun, captured during the assault on Alexandria in 1801, and a valued trophy, should no longer accompany the Regiment on its travels as it was 'a perpetual charge against the public'. The gun was given a permanent home at Woolwich; and in compensation, the 54th were permitted to carry 'Marabout' on their colours, and the name was substituted for 'Egypt' on the Sphinx. Since 'Marabout' was an honour unique to the Regiment, it was an exchange that was convenient as well as honourable. The gun was later returned and is now in the Regimental Museum.

The Irish troubles of 1842—the year the Regiment returned there—were the outcome of Dan O'Connell's agitation for 'Repeal of the Union' and the huge public meetings he was addressing up and down the country. 'On the sacred Hill of Tara', writes one Irish historian, 'it is said that a quarter of a million people listened to him'; a later demonstration, at Clontarf, was spiked by the presence of the 54th, and cancelled in consequence by O'Connell himself.

Civil disorders figure rather prominently on the 54th's agenda about this time. Their two years back in Gibraltar were uneventful; but in 1847 they were despatched to the West Indies, where the recently emancipated slaves were discovering that serfdom could not be ended by a stroke of the pen. The worst riot, at Castries in St. Lucia, in 1849, was well-handled by the Regiment under the command of Major Yorke Moore who, only the previous year, had rather surprisingly survived riding his horse over a 250-feet cliff in the nearby island of Dominica. The horse had been less lucky. The other hazards of life in the Antilles—ophthalmia, yellow jack, hurricanes and cheap rum, were still in evidence, but less virulent in their effects than they had been half a century before.

From the West Indies the Regiment went to Canada for three years, two of them in Quebec, and one at Kingston, Ontario. Colonel Fane was promoted to Major-General and left the Regiment after twenty-two years in command; and there was, strangely, more sickness than there had been in the West Indies, and, less strangely, a spate of desertions, America being the magnet. When the 54th were recalled on the outbreak of the Crimean War, no fewer than 150 men volunteered to stay—making Canada as popular as India for the serving soldier. But the remainder never got nearer Russia than Gibraltar; and by 1856 they were back in England, only to be summoned out east the following year to assist in suppressing the Indian Mutiny. They left the U.K. in three parties in different ships during the summer of 1857. Two reached the Hugli after uneventful voyages of four months: the third arrived, eventually, after a voyage that was anything but uneventful. The ship was a four-masted iron steamer of 1,300 tons displacement by the name of the *Sarah Sands*; and the 54th's party on board consisted of Headquarters, the Grenadiers, No. 5 and the Light Companies—14 officers, 354 NCOs and men and 11 women, all told. The CO was Lieutenant-Colonel Moffat; and they left Portsmouth on August 15.

One does not expect to come across an absolutely first-rate sea story among the records of a Regiment of the Line; but the voyage of the *Sarah Sands* to India with the 54th is just that; and, in fact, Kipling subsequently wrote of it

D.R.—5

in *Land and Sea Tales*. From the first, ominous loss of a man overboard on the passage to the Cape, to the baffling headwinds and a mutinous crew, it lacks nothing of menace or excitement.

But these were mere omens compared with what was to come; for on November 11, when the *Sarah Sands* was 800 miles north-east of Mauritius, on course for the Bay of Bengal and running before a freshening breeze, Sergeant Murray of the 54th saw smoke coming from the stern hatch. The alarm was raised; and as soon as it had been established that the fire was serious, the ship was turned head to wind, sail was struck, and boats lowered. These were intended for the women and sick; but the crew were over the side with the best, leaving Captain Castle, the Master, the ship's petty officers and firemen and the Regiment, to deal with the fire. Colonel Moffat, who had been helping the ladies into boats, was rowed away before he could scramble back aboard, and took no part in the subsequent proceedings except as a frustrated spectator.

The after hold was next to the magazines, which had been stocked for the Army in India, and the immediate task was to reach them before the fire. The starboard magazine was quickly cleared; but the port one was already full of smoke, adding the fear of asphyxiation to that of explosion. A party of volunteers with cloths over their faces struggled below; and slowly, barrel by barrel, the powder was man-handled on deck and thrown over the side. There were ninety barrels altogether, and they succeeded in extricating all but two. Those two—ship's stores, and separate from the rest—were to give a considerable incentive to the men on board during the next twelve hours—and probably saved the ship.

Despite unremitting efforts, the fire continued to spread. The coal in the bunkers was threatened, and the saloon, where the Colours had been hung on embarkation, was soon engulfed, the Colours themselves being saved in the nick

SS 'Sarah Sands', auxiliary screw iron steamship, 1300 tons, which caught fire in the Indian Ocean, November 11, 1857.

of time by one of the ship's quartermasters by the name of Richmond, helped by Private Wiles. Meanwhile a bucket-party, working in the suffocating heat and smoke below, drenched the coal and tried desperately, but vainly, to bring the fire under control. When a man passed out, his senseless body was dragged up on deck, and another man promptly took his place. But all was in vain.

At about 8 o'clock that evening a volcano of flame erupted through the upper deck; the mizzen mast went up like a torch and fell hissing into the sea, where it acted like a sea-anchor in reverse. The ship's head fell away, and the wind, veering astern, fanned the flames: Lance-Corporal McCallum hacked through the remaining rigging, the mast drifted clear, and another crisis was safely past. The crew in the boats, in the meantime, refused to take a hawser and haul the ship's head back into wind, preferring to rest on their oars at a safe distance. What they saw must have been awe-inspiring enough, for in the darkness, the iron plates of the ship's hull aft were glowing cherry-red, and the glare of the flames lit up the smoke that went billowing away on the wind. To those watchers in the boats, a thousand miles from land, it must have seemed that they were literally between the devil and the deep.

At midnight the thing that had been haunting their numbed minds happened: the two remaining barrels of powder went up like a fireworks factory. The explosion blew a hole in the ship's quarter and nearly put her entire stern section under. For a fearful minute, as the water gushed into her, it seemed she must go down; but she steadied at last; and, in fact, it was a disguised blessing, for it served to douse the fire as the bucket-parties could never have done.

And when dawn broke, though the after part of the ship was a gutted skeleton of twisted iron, the steering gear and binnacle had gone, and there was 20 feet of water in the well, she was still afloat, and the fire was out. The boats were recalled—and this time, they came—essential repairs were carried out, a jury mast rigged, and course—by an officer's pocket-compass—set for Mauritius, where they arrived ten days later.

Although the grimy and half-clothed survivors—and, amazingly, all had survived—were royally treated in Port Louis, their adventures were not quite over yet. The *Clarendon* which took them on to India had been used for carrying indentured labourers from the tropics, was alive with tarantulas and centipedes, and lacked any but the most primitive accommodation; and, to cap it all, they were struck by a typhoon, and the Master died of a heart attack. However, they got there—eventually.*

★ There are several accounts of 'The Burning of the *Sarah Sands*' by eyewitnesses, of which two—Lieutenant Frederick Schlotel's (1870) and Sergeant Murray's (1906) are similar, and in places identical. Far the raciest is by Private George Diggens

At all events, the 54th came out of it all with flying colours, and were the subject of a General Order by the Duke of Cambridge—inspired, it is said, by the Queen herself—which was read at the head of every regiment, commending them for their 'remarkable gallantry and resolution, presence of mind, high courage, coolness and discipline', the sort of encomium normally earned by a Regiment only after the most expensive of victories. A number of officers received accelerated promotion, the Royal Humane Society presented medals to Major Brett and Private Wiles and congratulations to all and sundry, and the men were promised an extra 3s. 6d. a week on their pensions.*

The Mutiny was still raging when the Regiment finally came together again early in 1858, though Lucknow had been relieved, and its reliever, 'Holy Havelock', who had once served briefly in the 39th, was dead. For the next two years, the Regiment was kept busy up and down the valleys of the Ganges and the Gogra; but, on the whole, the ill luck that had dogged them throughout their history persisted. The forts of Rhotas Gurh and Sirhoul frustrated them; they spent twelve hours on the mud in the Ganges while the arch mutineer, Koer Singh, gave them the slip; and they were left to guard Campbell's communications

---

(1906), who was the Doctor's servant. The crew he dismisses as 'foreigners and mutinous scoundrels'—and, needless to add, cowards; while his descriptions of the horror of that night are laced with a sententious philosophising that exactly fits the occasion and the period.

* There is one other odd footnote to this story. The V.C. was instituted in 1856: in 1858 the warrant was extended to cover acts of conspicuous courage and bravery under circumstances of extreme danger, not necessarily in the presence of the enemy, such as the occurrence of a fire on board a ship. The Colonel of the Regiment applied for an award of the Victoria Cross to be made to the Regiment. This was turned down, but the name of an individual was invited; that of Private Andrew Walsh—one of the magazine party—was submitted. However, this was again turned down on the grounds that 'the warrant of August 10, 1858, has on restrospective effect'.

while he methodically mopped up the rebel strongholds in Oudh. They lost a fortune in men through sickness—over 200 in two years; 381 in nine—and received no battle honour and precious few medals. But that was part of a soldier's lot, in India or anywhere else.

By the spring of 1866 they were home again, relieved the 39th at Manchester, and put in a two-year stint at Aldershot. The following year, the Colours which Quartermaster Richmond had rescued from the burning saloon of the *Sarah Sands* were ceremonially laid up in Norwich Cathedral. In 1949 these Colours were moved and laid up in Sherborne Abbey, where 36 other Colours of the Dorset Regiment are preserved. In 1868 old General Fane died at the age of 70. His connection with the Regiment spanned nearly forty years, and his place in their pantheon was secure.

That same year they were back in Ireland, mainly in the bogs of Connaught; and to complete the circuit, embarked for India in 1871. This was a very different passage from the previous occasion, for the Suez Canal was open, and the voyage took five weeks. The Cardwell system which had caused the 39th and the 75th to be linked now linked the 54th with the 95th Foot, whose territorial connection was with Derbyshire; similarly, this was no more than a brief *mariage de convenance*.

But Cardwell's reforms were part of what one would now call a new deal for the Army, and one which was to pension off into history the image of the despised, drunken and licentious soldiery. Training became more systematic and more thorough, and the boredom of barrack and canton-ment life was mitigated—and sobered—by the encourage-ment of games and athletics. Bedside lamps for the troops might still be a couple of generations away; but at least their lives were less nasty, brutish and short than in the past.

In 1877 the Regiment acquired the tempestuous, and stirrupless, light infantryman, Lord Mark Kerr as Colonel; and it was during his brief tenure that they were warned for duty in the 2nd Burma War. But with characteristic 54th luck, King Theebaw caved in soon after they arrived; and there was nothing for them but to kick their heels in Rangoon for twelve months.

Back in India in 1879–80, they received the first intimation of their impending amalgamation with the 39th; and on July 1, 1881, they officially ceased being the 54th Regiment of Foot, and became the 2nd Battalion, the Dorsetshire Regiment. On the previous night, at mess, the punch-bowl which the Duke of Kent had presented to them for their part in putting down the Gibraltar mutiny at Christmas, 1802, was filled; and a toast was drunk to the 54th. With the merging of these two 'fine old corps', the history of the Dorsets as such begins.

Chapter

10

1881–1914

WITH the birth of the Dorsetshire Regiment the normal peacetime establishment was fixed at two Regular, one Militia and one Volunteer Battalion; and, among all the other changes and adjustments which amalgamation entailed was a new badge which incorporated the outstanding honours of both the 39th and the 54th: the castle and key, with *Montis Insignia Calpe, Primus in Indis*, and the Sphinx, with Marabout. The two changes which were most resented were the disappearance of the old regimental numbers, and the introduction of white facings —common to all non-Royal English regiments—in place of green; though the latter were restored in 1904.

It had so happened that both Regiments—or battalions as they now became—were in India on amalgamation; but they did not remain together for long. The mild climate of Queen Victoria's later years was laced with minor wars in Egypt and the Sudan to which both battalions were, at one time or another, summoned, and which both contrived to miss. By 1893 the 1st were back in India; while the 2nd, true to the 54th's talent for finding itself off the map, sent a detachment to Crete in 1898 to deal with those felicitously named brigands, the Bashi-Bazouks, who were busy putting the local Christians to the sword; and if the troops suffered more discomfort than action, that too was in the 54th's traditions. They had never been a lucky regiment, though with Kruger brandishing his brand-new Mausers on the borders of the Transvaal and the Orange Free State, they had some stirring times ahead of them. More of that later; for in India, the 1st Battalion had troubles of their own. First came the Moplahs—the Bashi-Bazouks, one might say, of that Malabar coast where the 39th had dealt so summarily with the Rajah of Coorg in 1837—who were themselves dealt with summarily in 1894. Three years later, the Afridis and Orakzais on the North West Frontier, who had been in a state of rebellion for half a dozen years, came together with most of the other Pathan tribes to set off the most serious rising the Frontier had ever known; and in the autumn of 1897 the 1st Battalion joined the Tirah Field Force with its 40,000 pack-animals and set out to march into those bleak, unfriendly hills.

The first real clash came at Dargai, a high ridge guarded by steep cliffs and only accessible via a spur wide open to the enemy's fire. The individual companies of the 2nd Gurkhas and Dorsets which attempted to cross the spur and rush the Pathan sangars were badly cut up; and it was during one of these ill-advised dashes that Private Vickery went out and brought in a wounded comrade under fire: an action which, combined with some stirring work later, earned him the VC. The position was eventually carried by the Gordons, reinforcing the Gurkhas, the Dorsets and the Derbys with strong artillery support; and a grim spot it proved during the night that followed.

Although the valleys of the Afridis' heartland were milder and in some ways, more hospitable, forage parties usually had to fight their way back to camp, and snipers forced the men into dug-outs at night. The next serious engagement came at Saran Sar in November, and involved the battalion in a sticky fighting withdrawal; but they were taking the measure of their elusive and ubiquitous enemy by now, and succeeded in disengaging with very light losses. For a month thereafter, the Afridi villages were given a taste of Her Majesty's displeasure; and then, in December, the force pulled out. It was cold and wet, with occasional snow, in those wind-blistered mountain valleys, and the Afridis hung on their flanks by day and night, exacting what

revenge they could; and no one can have been sorry to
reach Peshawar. Apart from Vickery's VC, the battalion
gained a DSO and two DCMs, and the regiment a Battle
Honour.

The 2nd Battalion was in England when the South
African War started, were fully mobilised by November

*Corporal Sam Vickery, VC—a somewhat highly coloured version of
the hero (standing, centre) with his Queen. The seated figure is thought
to be Piper Findlater of the Gordon Highlanders, who was also
awarded the VC at Dargai for continuing to play his pipes though
shot in both ankles.*

1899, and were in South Africa in time to hear of the 'Black Week' during which, among other misfortunes, Buller's first attempt to relieve Ladysmith had come to grief at Colenso. The khaki uniform, which the 1st Battalion had scorned so bitterly back in the '80s, was now accepted—though it might be 'anything from canary to puce' in colour—for this was the first of the twentieth-century wars as well as the last of the nineteenth century.

The battalion landed at Durban, and was whipped straight to the scene of operations on the Tugela River. Early in the new year Buller was ready to try again; and the battalion, as part of Warren's 5th Division, advanced on January 10. To begin with all went reasonably well, in spite of heavy rain. The main force crossed the Tugela at Trichard's Drift, while the Dorsets took part in a diversionary attack downstream. This time the attempt broke down with the expensive series of misunderstandings known as Spion Kop, on the spur of which the Dorsets spent a weary and unprofitable day. With its abandonment Buller pulled his whole army back across the Tugela to think again; and the inhabitants of Ladysmith reset their mouse-traps.

Buller's third attempt, at Vaal Krantz, never got off the ground, and, for a week, his fourth seemed doomed also as the 2nd Somerset L.I. and the Dorsets vainly confronted the Boers in their rocky stronghold on Grobelaar Kloof. There, among the kopjes to the north of Colenso, in the heat and the rain and the snipers' bullets, they remained, while Buller at last switched his main attack to his right, and within twenty-four hours broke the Boer line and opened the road to Ladysmith, which was relieved on March 3.

The battalion went into the outpost line north of the town, where they received, besides regular reinforcements, a Volunteer Service Company fresh from England; and in May Buller's measured advance northward along the border between Natal and the OFS continued. After a quick success at Botha's Pass, the next objective was Alleman's Nek, in the northern Drakensberg, where the Boers had rallied. The British force came up with them on June 10, and launched their attack the following day. The description in the Official History of the action that followed—very much of a Dorsets' affair—cannot be bettered.

> 'Four thousand yards away across a smooth and open bowl of grass, along the bottom of which wound the dry bed of a spruit, Alleman's Nek rose abruptly in two cliffs or bluffs, between which the road climbed by a glacis totally destitute of cover to the indentation which carried it over the summit. Below the western rampart of the Nek . . . lay two small kopjes, separated from the main feature by a ravine wherein were many riflemen and a gun.' On the eastern side, and in front of the plateau, 'stood up like a barbican a tall conical kopje, connected to a similarly shaped peak upon the mass behind by a deeply-bowed saddle . . . some two thousand Boers being upon the position from end to end.
> 'The objective of the left battalion, the Dorsets, was the conical outwork from which poured a heavy fire . . . The Dorsetshire Regiment, followed at 300 yards distance by the Middlesex, attacked with resolution, and without a check, though the slopes were steep, and a wire fence at the bottom of the valley had been marked as a range by the Boer riflemen. At 3.40 pm the summit of the cone was rushed, the shells from the heavy [British] guns bursting in the enemy's lines only a few feet from the foremost rank of the assault.'

The next objective was the saddle and the second conical hill, both of which were under heavy fire; and Colonel Law ordered the reserve company to charge across the former.

> 'The assault was brilliantly delivered. Advancing by a succession of short charges, the Dorsetshire Regiment,

well supported by the Middlesex, swept across the
intervening saddle, carried the near kopje, and clambering
up the rugged precipice behind, were upon the main
crest-line by 5.0 pm, the enemy flying before them. . . .
After nightfall, therefore, the Boers drew off and left
Sir Redvers Buller's troops in sole occupation of the
last portal into the Transvaal.'

The Dorsets' advance, which cost them 12 killed and
52 wounded, was 'a marvel of steadiness and good discipline', said an officer of the supporting brigade; and the
importance of the victory at that stage of the war was
undoubted. It was part of a pattern of defeat for the Boers
during 1900 which caused them finally to give up trying to
keep an army in the field, and turn instead to guerrilla
warfare.

The Dorsets' share in this tedious and frustrating
business was typical of the infantryman's lot in South
Africa from 1900 to 1902; in that vast and rolling country,
with an enemy born to the saddle, the train and the horse
had the edge; and the foot-soldier's job tended to be the
largely static one of guarding the railways, with an occasional stint of convoying guns or prisoners or stock; or
marching immense distances to try—usually in vain—to
trap a reported concentration of Boers. One of these
occurred in July, when the Dorsets drove a party of them
off Gras Kop; another in September; and again, at
Wakerstroom in November, when they were based at
Ingogo in Natal.

In November Kitchener took over supreme command
from Roberts, and set about the difficult and repulsive task
of bringing the country and its scattered inhabitants into
subjection. The prime objective was President Steyn's
mobile republican government; and it was partly in the
hope of nabbing them that, in April 1901, General Bullock
made a sweep through the south-eastern Transvaal.
Despite more than a month on trek, and a deal of skirmish-

F Company, 2nd Dorsets, at de Wet's Farm, June 1900, before marching through Botha's Pass into the Orange Free State.

ing—cold, hunger and the Boer habit of setting the grass on fire were some of the regular tribulations—the column's haul amounted to a mere 30 prisoners and 180 waggons. Similar sweeps in June and July met with similar results. They did rather better in August, with two columns working in harness, capturing 50 prisoners, 200 waggons and 35,000 head of stock; less well in September, their last before being shifted to the blockhouse line, north of Bloemfontein.

These lines, dividing the country up into a pattern of wired enclosures, were designed to hamper the movement of the commandos: manning the intervening strongpoints was monotonous work. Occasionally a party of Boers would demonstrate against a blockhouse to cover the passage of a commando through the wire; as often, the alarm was set off by an owl upsetting the arrangement of tin cans on the wire, to turn out the troops in a fever of dry-mouthed anticipation. It was all a part of this ill-matched war, where a quarter of a million British and Imperial troops well over half on static, line of communication duties, were mocked for two full years by no more than 20,000 farmers on horseback in the field at any time; and one is reminded of Burgoyne's unfortunate remark about the '10,000 peasants' during the American War of Independence.

A detachment from the battalion had, quite early on, become part of the 5th Division, Mounted Infantry; and they had a rather more interesting time of it, notably during Louis Botha's irruption into Natal in September 1901. The Boers attacked Fort Prospect and Itala, but were repelled by the two greatly outnumbered garrisons; a setback which clinched Botha's decision to abandon his advance. At the former, Captain Rowley, who had done brilliantly at Alleman's Nek, distinguished himself again, had a narrow escape when a bullet went through his helmet, and won a DSO. His name, and that of Colonel Law, who had had thirty-three years with the Regiment when he left it in 1902, stand out in the battalion's records of the South African War. The Regimental History, summing up the work of the MI, says: 'There were indeed few parts of the theatre of war the Dorsets did not visit sooner or later'.

In March 1902 the battalion moved to another stretch of line, east of Pretoria, where there was even less doing; but they had only been there a couple of months when the war was brought to a close by the Treaty of Vereeniging, signed on May 31; by October, the whole battalion, bar a few who had been transferred to the 1st in India, were home.

The officers and men of the 2nd Battalion had gained between them one CB (to Colonel Law), 4 DSOs, 15 DCMs, any number of 'Mentions' and two Battle Honours: Relief of Ladysmith and South Africa. Their casualties had, on the whole, been light: 21 had been killed, 63 had died of disease and 100 had been wounded. On arrival in England they were stationed at Portland; and their route there, via Dorchester, became something of a triumphal march.

The 1st Battalion's further nine years in India after the Tirah campaign were quiet, with little to vary the routine of the hot weather move to the Hills, the cold weather manoeuvres and exercises on the plains. When the battalion became due for home service in 1906, no less than 700 NCOs and men were transferred to the 2nd Battalion—which was just arriving in India—and only 378 returned to England.

Their spell at home included strike duty at Willesden Junction, the presentation of new Colours by King George V, the first manoeuvres—in 1912—in which aircraft ever co-operated with the Army; and an unpleasant spell in an Ireland brought to the boil by the Home Rule Bill, and the fulminations of Carson's Ulster Volunteers.

Under the general reorganisation of 1907 the Dorsetshire Regiment now consisted of the two regular battalions, the 3rd (Special Reserve—formerly Militia) Battalion, and the 4th (Territorial—formerly Volunteer) Battalion. The 1st Battalion, still in its tour at home, had become part of the Fifth Division, and was thus on call for France as soon as war broke out on August 4, 1914.

Chapter

II

1914–1918

THE Dorsetshire Regiment had a total of 12 battalions of one kind or another, at one time or another, during the First World War, of which six saw active service. From the dense and intricate details of their activities through four years of war, certain actions and events are illuminated as by starshell, and will be recounted in due course; but, briefly, the 1st, 5th and 6th Battalions served in France—the 1st throughout, the other two from 1916–18; the 2nd, with the 54th's luck still haunting them, were wiped out at Kut, but, re-raised, fought in Palestine, as did the 2/4th. The 5th came in for the last miserable five months

New boys: volunteers for the 5th Dorsets, August 1914.
D.R.—6

of the Gallipoli campaign before going to France; and the
1/4th repeated history, in a way, by being the first Territorial
Battalion to serve in India, before going on to Mesopotamia
in 1916. The remaining six battalions—the 3rd, the
Territorial (Home Service), the 1st Volunteer, the 7th, and
the two Garrison battalions, were employed on various
useful, if unspectacular, duties at home.

★

The 1st Battalion sailed for France as part of the BEF
on August 14, 1914, and were in action nine days later at
Mons. They did what they could against overwhelming
numbers, extricated themselves from among the slagheaps,
and retreated in good order the 150 miles back to the
Marne. It was baking hot; the roads were clogged with
stragglers; all round them men were ditching all their
equipment except their waterbottles; it is in such circumstances of desperation and despair that a regiment's
quality is tested, and the 1st Battalion, toughened by four
years of iron command by the famous Lieutenant-Colonel
Chichester, came through it all unbroken, and ready for
the counter-offensive in early September. They recrossed
the Aisne with surprising ease, and dug in with the river
at their backs and a dauntingly superior enemy force in
front.*

With the frustration of the Schlieffen Plan, the Germans
made for the Channel; and the BEF was transferred to
Flanders, where the remnants of its original battalions—
and many hundreds more not yet even recruited—were to
spend much of the next four years. This British advance
in the autumn was a dogged, costly affair: at La Bassée,
in October, the 50 casualties included the 2nd-in-Command,
Major Roper; at Pont-Fixe next day, in stopping a savage

---

* The 1st Battalion's CO in 1914 was Lieutenant-Colonel L. J.
Bols (ex-Devons), later Lieutenant-General Sir Louis. He was
Lord Allenby's Chief of Staff in Palestine, 1917–18. Lieutenant-
Colonel Chichester, later Major-General Sir Arlington, was
Colonel of the Regiment from 1922–33.

German counter-attack, the battalion lost 15 officers and
320 men, and the survivors of three companies were just
enough to make up one—to earn the mention of 'the fine
fighting of the Dorsets' from Lord French—a day of two
later they lost another 140, then 100—and so it went on,
until the advance finally foundered in the November mud
on the Messines ridge with sixteen consecutive days of
enemy shelling. By the beginning of December the war in
the west had set in the siege-pattern that was not to be
broken until March 1918; and the BEF—with the Dorsets
—settled down to the first miseries of trench warfare in the
Ypres Salient. 'By the end of October 1914', wrote one
officer, 'the old army which had borne the burden and heat
of those terrible days of the first August of the war had
passed away.' And Major C. H. D. Ward, writing the
war-time history of the 1st Battalion, suggests several
reasons why. 'In all this fighting the BEF had always
found themselves opposed to superior numbers, better
equipped. The British Army was the first to use the
machine-gun, and was the last to be fully equipped with it.'
Battalions had two only; and for bombs were driven to
rely on home-made contraptions 'the danger of which was
shared by those who fired them'.

That first winter there was considerable scope for trying
out these home-made explosives, for each side kept up
what harassment it could; but for the Dorsets the first real
test of 1915 came at Hill 60. This spoil-heap from a railway
cutting had been lost in December, and was retaken, with
the Dorsets' help, on the last day of April. Next day they
relieved the Devons; and that evening the Germans attacked
with gas. This was not the first gas-attack—it had been
used against the French ten days previously—but 'pro-
tection' consisted merely of bits of flannel or gauze; and the
horror of Hill 60 is heightened by the fact that the German
trenches were only forty yards away, and the British could
clearly see the nozzles discharging the chlorine, which

drifted across towards them in a thick white and yellow cloud.

The men's instinct was to drop into their trenches, and this was fatal, for the gas was heavier than air and collected in dense and deadly concentration in every hollow. One officer, Lieutenant Kestell-Cornish, grasped this, seized a rifle, jumped on to the parapet and 'calling to his men to do the same, opened fire into the cloud'. 'The men who did this', reported the Brigadier, 'were hardly affected by the gas'. All too few had the wit or courage to do so; and that night 'the deep and narrow trenches were blocked with dead, with many others dying in terrible agony'. Among all the commonplace horrors of war—and even of trench war— the use of gas still has something of the power to stir the disgust and anger which drove one Dorset officer to write: 'Clean killing is at least comprehensive [sic] but this murder by slow agony absolutely knocks me. The whole civilised world ought to rise up and exterminate those swine across the hill.'

The attack on Hill 60, to which the gas was a preliminary, was driven off—not least, perhaps, because the wind changed and some of it drifted back upon those who sent it—but a few days later the Germans tried again. This time they were more successful, and the battalion lost 170 men—among them the CO, Colonel Cowie, one of the battalion's unforgotten heroes—in attempting to keep them off what was 'a mere rubbish heap of shell and mine-torn earth, timber and dead bodies' in which the British trenches were nothing but 'shapeless cavities'.

Hill 60 was lost, and with it 627 men of the battalion in one abominable week. For another two and a half months they remained in the area, and then moved south to the relatively quiet Somme front—at about the moment when the 6th Battalion arrived in France. And there, with the war a year old, we will leave them, in their 'deep and well-constructed trenches which were really quite comfortable'—

The original caption reads: 'Advance of the gallant Dorsets near Basra. Of the 18 miles of their route, 9 miles were under water.' This advance took place during the battle of Shaiba, which was fought under flood conditions.

comfort being as relative as quiet—and turn to the activities of the other battalions.

★

The 2nd, which had started its spell in India in 1906, was still there when war broke out; but in October 1914, with Turkey obviously about to enter the war on the German side, they took ship for the Persian Gulf and the threatened oilfields. By mid-November they were on the move to Basra, with rain, sodden ground, and considerable Turkish opposition to contend with, notably at Sahil on November 15, which cost the Dorsets 170 casualties, but cost the Turks Basra, which they evacuated. The British force entered that 'labyrinth of incredibly dirty and evil-smelling streets' at the end of the month.

During the advance north sporadic contact was made with the Turks, and the 'one-minute battle' of Nukheila, though of no strategic importance, is so vivid in the telling it deserves a mention. A force of cavalry, despatched as a diversion, had been intercepted by a strong force of Arab irregulars, and been forced to retreat upon Nukheila, where the Dorsets were drawn up, ready to support them.

'So great was their panic', wrote one eyewitness, 'that they did not see the clear road nearly 300 yards in breadth which we had left between the two lines . . . but went so far as to jump over us lying on the ground.* The Arabs were so close to our own men that they were within 30 yards of us before we could open fire. Then we let them have it very hot and strong. You never saw such a surprised lot of human beings, and our fire stopped them in about 15 yards; a minute later there was not an Arab to be seen.'

It is an episode out of one of Victoria's tribal wars misplaced in time; with the sun and the dust, the galloping horses and the limbers hopping and lurching over the sand, the cordite smoke and the ever-present mirage on the horizon, the Arabs thundering in the wake of the guns, and the two stolid lines of British infantry holding their fire until they could safely let that point-blank broadside loose; one can hear the shouts and the shots, the thudding of hooves and the screams of dying horses, and smell the powder and the sweat.

There were other actions, of which the sharp little battle of Ahwaz against a mass of Arab horse showed the Dorsets at their most stubborn and won them eight DCMs; then, in April 1915, the main Turkish force, recently reinforced, attacked the advanced British outpost of Shaiba. They were repulsed, and the following day the British counter-attacked. After taking several of the enemy's outposts with relative ease, they ran into concentrated fire and were slowed to a crawl. With the last reserves in the line, and the outcome 'an absolute toss-up', the Dorsets got to their weary feet, licked their parched lips, and charged across the 200 yards of open ground between them and the Turks. This clinched it. The rest of

* 'Needless to add that the cavalry were Indian, not British', the author, Lieutenant D. A. Simmons, adds needlessly. *The Story of my Experiences . . . in Mesopotamia*, unpublished, is in the Regimental Museum: it is replete with unconscious superiorities of this kind.

Mesopotamia, 1915–1916. 1/4th Dorsets on their way up the Tigris—one of the superb collection of photographs by A. J. Garland of the 2nd Dorsets discovered in the Regimental archives.

the line followed, and the Turks began scrambling out of the first line of trenches in flight; soon the second line was cleared as well. The day was won, and the road to Kut—and, ironically, eventual captivity for the battalion—was open.

'I don't think I have ever been so unutterably weary,' wrote Simmons, 'or had such a raging, unquenchable thirst.' The battalion lost 15 officers, including the CO, Colonel Rosher, and 152 men killed or wounded; won 7 DCMs for gallantry, and a battle honour which is included among the ten 'Great War Honours' on the King's Colour of the Regiment. Another DCM went to RSM J. R. H. Bolingbroke, then in the Norfolks. 'Bolly' was wounded at Kut and evacuated; was transferred to the

Regiment in 1916, and later became a commissioned quartermaster, and was awarded the MBE. He is still alive, aged 86.

Shaiba is an evocative battle in several ways, and not least in its combining of the old infantry style—in the tradition of Albuera—with trenches and machine-guns. Nukheila was a picture-book battle from the Imperial past: Shaiba was of its time, and yet one with the long history of infantry valour.

After some months spent mostly in Amara, the battalion 'covered themselves with glory' at the Northern Redoubt which they took at bayonet-point, during the assault on Kut in September, and did it again at the battle of Ctesiphon in November. 'In all my experience of war', wrote Townshend, 'I have never seen or heard of anything so fine as the deliberate and tranquil advance of the thin chain of Dorsets, in extended order, moving south from V.P.'* Victory seemed assured, but the climax of this extremely savage battle was still to come. General Townshend was forced to put in all his reserves to meet a succession of dogged attacks by the Turkish Anatolian 51st Division. 'They came back to the attack with a great gust of fire', wrote one officer, 'that swept down on us like a storm in the Himalayas', and actually entered the British trenches, only to be driven out again by the specially trained Dorset bombers. It was a Pyrrhic victory, and proved to be the turning point of the campaign. General Townshend had lost 4,500 men all told; the Dorsets 243, or nearly half their strength. Far from advancing to Baghdad— a proposition the validity of which Townshend himself had had doubts of from the start—he was forced to make a fighting retreat back to Kut, which he re-entered on December 3 after what one officer described as a far worse ordeal than the retreat from Mons.

* In *My Campaign in Mesopotamia*. General Townshend was GOC 6th Indian Division.

Townshend and his men were now beleaguered well inside enemy-held territory, with very little chance of being able to break out. With the coming of the winter floods this chance vanished entirely: their only hope of salvation now lay with the relieving force which set out under General Aylmer in mid-December. With that force was one battalion unknown to the Army Council: it was known as 'The Norsets', and we shall come to the fate of both of them and the garrison inside Kut later on.

★

Of the other battalions of the Regiment during that first year of the war, the 3rd was stationed at Wyke Regis, doing guard duty and acting as a pool and filter for reinforcements bound for the Western Front; and the 4th was divided into two. The 2/4th remained for the time being in England, while the 1/4th sailed for India in October '14. There they remained, mainly on guard duty at the aliens' internment camp at Ahmednagar, until in early 1916 they were sent to Mesopotamia.

The 5th Battalion, raised in the first month of the war as part of 'K1'—the First New Army—trained in England, and a year later formed part of General Stopford's army which landed at Suvla Bay in the final attempt to resolve the impasse on the Gallipoli Peninsula. There is not much to be said of this curiously supine assault, for it was all of a piece with the rest of that disastrous sideshow. At first, after certain navigational problems had been overcome— the lighters that did not land on the wrong beach went aground offshore—the troops had it all their own way, and given 'the resolution and initiative that were conspicuously lacking' might well have achieved what they set out to do. Instead, however, so desultory was their advance, thanks to the vacillations of the command, that the Turks had time to muster reinforcements, and each of the three attempts to capture the vital high ground inland was a failure. During the third of these, south of Chocolate Hill, the battalion lost over 300 men in attack and counter-attack.

Thereafter, the operation came to a halt; the heat of September dissolved in the gales and rains of autumn, the blizzards of winter, as they stuck it out on the ridge of Karakol Dagh. By the time they were evacuated, on December 16, the battalion was in a parlous state, and temporarily unfit for active service. It was a melancholy end to the one really imaginative strategic plan of those four most frustrating years.

★

And so, throughout 1916 and 1917, the stalemate which Gallipoli had been intended to break, continued virtually unchanged and unchangeable, no matter how many men died in its threnody of battles. The 1st and 6th Battalions in the line round Ypres, or on the Somme, were joined in France in July 1916 by the 5th. All were swallowed up in the mighty military machine on the Western Front, whose numbers rose from 270,000 in December 1914 to a million a year later, and 1,343,000 when the 5th arrived.

Out of it all certain vivid pictures emerge, such as this description of a raid near Albert in the Ancre valley, by the 1st Battalion during 1916.

'The night was still to a degree which no night had been before. The broken posts and wire which marked the boundaries of No Man's Land and the white chalk of the mine craters were agleam in the moonlight, and it was so clear that I could discern the ruins and broken tree stumps of the village. Yet no shot was fired while a hundred men crawled through our wire into shell holes in front. Behind them the trenches were lined with men, for the "stand to arms" had been passed down . . . Then at last the silence was broken by a machine gun firing from the dim ruins of Orvillers, and sweeping our parapets from end to end. Then again there was silence. . . . Time! The mine exploded . . . The earth throbbed.

Then again, but for one moment only, there was an unearthly stillness. This was succeeded by a weird sound like rustling leaves . . . then, with the noise of a hurricane, the shells passed, and the whole outline of the German positions was seared with the appalling lightning and thunder of our artillery.'

Of the Somme, Major-General G. N. Wood, who was with the 1st Battalion, writes: 'July 1st 1916 is a hateful memory for the bulk of the British Army, and among them, the 1st Dorsets. Like that of so many others, its attack was a complete failure against a scientific German defence, though honour was saved by the fact that a handful of our men reached, and held on, in the front line of the Leipzig Redoubt'. And of two raids in the early part of 1917, General Wood writes: 'Both were, very wrongly, accompanied by a beloved Brigadier, General Lumsden, VC, attended by our ex-bandmaster, Richards, who at a mature

Imperial War Museum
Battle of Ypres, 1917. Men of the Dorsets resting and cleaning rifles in the ruins of a farm near Langemarck.

age had insisted on laying down his baton to become a combatant subaltern, until Lumsden, seeing his "good grey head", had appointed him to his staff'.

In the valley of the Ancre that winter the mud was up to a man's waist; trench foot was as rife as scurvy in the old Navy; men died by bullet and shell, by pneumonia and fever and drowning; and the passage of years brought no alleviation beyond a spell out of the line and in billets or the blessing of a 'blighty'. The battles in which the Dorsets fought and died are only names today: The Bluff, Fricourt, Lesboeufs, Mametz Wood, Gouzeaucourt, Thiepval: who remembers the courage and the suffering now of those mud-foundered middle years of the war?

*

More easily apprehensible was the equally wretched fate of the 2nd Battalion, isolated in Kut, which the winter rains and the rising Tigris had turned into an island. The defenders dug thirty miles of trenches at high speed; but after three frustrated attacks in December, the Turks contented themselves with investing the town—which was not difficult—and simply starving the garrison into surrender. This policy was partly dictated by the need to stave off the relieving force, which was struggling up the flooded Tigris valley, and partly by the floods which restrained the besiegers as much as the besieged. For both sides, the winter months were a constant battle against flood-water, which inundated British and Turkish trenches alike, and were only restrained from swamping the entire area to the north and west of the town by the 'bunds' or embankments, which required constant attention—'hours of back-breaking work on those awful bunds' as one of the survivors put it.

Rations were first reduced in January: by March the garrison were down to 1 lb. of mule and about a pound of barley bread a day, with an occasional starling as a *bonne bouche*. Milk, tea, sugar, eggs, cheese and jam had long since disappeared; and on April 24 only the emergency rations were left, and General Townshend knew that the siege could not be prolonged for more than another day or two. The failure of the *Julnar* to run the blockade with supplies the following day, in conjunction with the failure of the relieving force to break through the Turkish defences, made it inevitable.

Among that force was the 'Composite British Battalion', composed of drafts for the Norfolks and Dorsets and known as the Norsets; and they acquitted themselves well during the long hard slog towards Kut. Three times that April they reached Sannaiyat—so close that the garrison could hear the firing and thought that relief had arrived; but every time—during the night of April 17/18, the Turks put in a furious counter-attack which cost them 4,000 casualties and the final throw, three days later, was no more successful—their advance was stopped, as much by the floods as by a shortage of artillery. On April 27 Townshend asked for terms.

But the sufferings of the battalion were by no means over. 1,200 of the garrison's 1,500 sick were allowed to leave in an exchange of prisoners; the rest were marched, under conditions of appalling indifference and cruelty the thousand miles into the heart of Anatolia—to Afion-Kara-Hissar—and set to work. There are several accounts of that fearsome journey; but two, one by 2nd Lieutenant Simmons, whom we have quoted before, the other by RQMS F. A. Harvey, provide a tragic contrast between the treatment meted out by the Turks to officers and men. Not that the officers had an exactly comfortable time of it; but at Mosul, Simmons notes, 'they sent us up some food from the restaurant'; and although they were compelled to cross Asia Minor six to a cart, at Aleppo the Commandant 'quite understood our reluctance to living in the rooms allotted to us (they were alive with bugs), and he gave orders that we should be quartered at one of the hotels'.

Harvey's* account of the troops' progress is somewhat more harrowing, however. 'No rations of any kind were issued this day' he notes on May 11 'so we lay hungry on the desert for the night'. A week later: '. . . it had taken $6\frac{1}{2}$ hours to draw four dried dates and about 3 ounces of rice per man'; on May 24: 'Several men had lost their boots . . . their sufferings were terrible, their feet were horribly cut about'; on the 28th: 'Sergeant-Major Thomson was flogged by Mahomed Russi [the sadistic lieutenant in charge of the column] today'; on June 5th—the day they left Mosul— 'We had dropped a sprinkling of men along the road all the way along the march; these men had fallen out overcome by exhaustion and were never seen again. If they did not die by the roadside the Arabs would very soon be along and cut their throats for the sake of their boots.' And so on. Anyone who lagged was automatically flogged by the escort; and on one occasion their precious water-bags were maliciously punctured. On June 20 Harvey writes: 'The number we have left looks appalling; no one will ever know how many were left on the road side to die'.

And that was six months before they reached their final destination. None of the officers perished; but out of 350 Dorsets who set out from Kut, only 70 ever saw England again.

*

Kut had fallen, but the Mesopotamian campaign was not over, and two Dorset battalions were involved in the later, very successful operations. The 1/4th joined from India in February 1916, and fought two hard battles—at Ramadi and Khan Baghdadi—on the road to Baghdad; while the Dorset half of the Norsets became, in July, the 2nd (Provisional) Battalion, the Dorsetshire Regiment, and were mainly

---

* Harvey himself survived, to be killed—as Lieutenant and QM—in the Moplah troubles of 1921.

involved in guarding General Maude's communications during his advance which brought him to Baghdad in March 1917. However, there remained a strong Turkish force in the Jebel Hamrin range to the north; and the battalion was part of the 9th Brigade which was sent to deal with it.

In three tremendous forced marches, covering 85 miles in five days—they got themselves into that shocking country of ravine and hill; and there, on March 25, they ran into stiff and skilful opposition, followed by sniper infiltration and fierce counter-attacks. Two platoons were annihilated; a third escaped with their skins; and the survivors were ordered to retire. They succeeded in extricating themselves under heavy fire, and by dark they were back exactly where they had started from—or those who were left out of 500; the battalion lost 220 men at Jebel Hamrin, including some of its best officers and men.

After this bitter experience they had a quiet time of it for the remainder of the year; and in March 1918 they were transferred to Palestine, where the 2/4th had arrived seven months earlier.

At that time—mid '17—the British were holding a line south-east of Gaza, and Allenby had just taken over as C-in-C. At the beginning of November the third battle of Gaza began—and this time it was to be well and truly won. But before the town fell on the 7th, the 2/4th had to beat off three very determined Turkish attacks, preceded by massive artillery bombardments. Once it had fallen, Palestine lay open, and the Dorsets set off in pursuit of the retreating Turks—'an interesting series of operations in open warfare', as one officer described it. As always, there was a certain gruesome satisfaction in overrunning positions which had been closed and hostile for so long, a gruesomeness enhanced by the many mummified corpses which littered the Turkish salient.

By mid-November, cold, wet and miserable, the Dorsets had their first glimpse of Jerusalem through the rain, and found themselves beset in Nebi Samwil—that home of the prophet—which had just fallen to the men of the DCLI and Outram's Rifles. The Turks fought hard to regain it, and actually reached the courtyard of the mosque before being driven back by the cold steel of the 3/3rd Gurkhas with the support of the battalion. When, shortly afterwards, the 2/4th were relieved, they were greeted on their arrival at Junction Station by a West Indian fife and drum band— a nice touch in that land which was as strange—and as familiar—to both.

They had a wet and unpleasant Christmas in the Judean hills, a brisk adventure at Deir Ballut in March '18, when they were called upon to charge up the steep slopes of the wadi with fixed bayonets, and a tough battle in and around Berukin during Allenby's attempt to roll up the Turkish line from Berukin to the sea. In the struggle to take and hold Three Bushes Hill the Dorsets were fighting and marching for almost four days without a break; but then, just as everything was poised for the next advance, the Germans launched their March offensive on the Western Front, and Allenby was stripped of several divisions. His final campaign against the Turks was held up until September; but when it came it was decisive.

Both the recreated 2nd and the 2/4th Battalions were involved in the initial phases—the 2nd's performance at the Battle of Brown Hill, and on the Nablus road were memorable—and by mid-October the Allies were in Damascus. On October 31, anticipating the Germans by less than a fortnight, the Turks agreed to an armistice.

The 2nd spent an unhappy six months in Damascus before returning to England in June 1919; the 2/4th moved to Egypt, where in that same year, they had a rebellion to contend with until, on disbandment, they gradually returned home for demobilisation.

★

The year 1918 on the Western Front falls naturally into two contrasting periods: the German offensive which started on March 21, drove two huge salients into the Allied line, and nearly carried the Germans—for the second time—to Paris: and Foch's counter-offensive, launched four months later, which carried the Allies—for the first time—to the Rhine, and so to victory.

'A season of "wind-up" set in', wrote the historian of the 5th Battalion on March 18. 'Day after day we heard the news of the Boche offensive all along the line . . . Any morning might see a host of grey-clad soldiers creeping across the plain. But they never came'. And indeed, until their transfer from the Loos salient to the area of Cambrai—where they were fully occupied at the Canal de Nord—the stirring events of 1918 largely passed them by.

But the 'wind-up' was well-founded, as the 6th discovered, being right in the route of the German thrust near Havrincourt Wood. Against the eight German divisions concentrated in that sector, the three British divisions could do nothing but contest every foot of ground, and then fall back; at one time the component parts of the battalion were as much as seven miles apart. 'Haggard, dead tired, depleted; but never broken', to quote the battalion history, they came together twenty-five miles back, having lost 250 men during the retreat.

But the German impetus ran out, and during the summer months the new line was stabilised, and the Allies built up their forces—strengthened now by United States troops—for the counter-stroke. It started badly for the 1st Battalion at Amiens in August, when they lost 300 and 'it seemed a miracle that the whole battalion was not decimated on the starting-line'; continued well for the 6th ten days later when they crossed the Ancre and advanced twenty miles in three weeks. 'The whole mood and atmosphere of battle were now changing,' wrote one officer; and in truth the

mould of the preceding four years was broken at last, and a war of movement restored.*

The assault on the Hindenburg Line—behind which the Germans had concentrated in 1917—followed in mid-September. At the crossing of the Selle the 6th were involved in one of 17 division's 'hardest and most successful battles'; and the 1st had their hour of glory at the St. Quentin canal, and again in the capture of the village of Sequehart; while both 1st and 6th were in action during the final battle of the war at the Sambre. 'My chief memory of the 1st Dorsets', writes General Wood, 'is their complete professionalism, which never wavered, even in the worst days . . .' Even after the Somme, and the appalling winter that followed, 'morale and offensive spirit never faltered, and the atmosphere was comradely and grimly cheerful'.

'It is customary to raise monuments to the dead', wrote the historian of the 1st Battalion, 'and, very rightly, to inscribe thereon the names of those who made the supreme sacrifice; but the Dorsets' Roll of Honour is the Regimental Roll'. For a regiment that had had its full share of death and glory, and was awarded forty-eight battle honours ranging from Shaiba to the Somme, it provides a just and generous epigraph.

* Sir Winston Churchill, writing in 1939, thought this final advance to be one of the "four supreme achievements" of the British Army, "along with Crécy, Blenheim and Waterloo."

Chapter 12

1919–1939

WITH the end of the war the Regiment swiftly resumed its normal peacetime composition of two regular battalions and one Territorial battalion—the 4th Dorsets—which evolved out of the disbanded 1/4th. The 3rd (Special Reserve) ceased to exist in 1919 and was not revived. With a plethora of officers some odd things happened; battalion commanders considered themselves lucky to have a platoon, and ex-brigadiers had to be content to command a company. After all the upheavals of the war things took a little time to settle down.

The first specific call on the Regiment's services—apart from the routine tasks of the occupation of Germany—was to assist in the relief of the British force which had been despatched to North Russia in 1918; and a mixed battalion, which included Hampshires, Somersets, Wiltshires and 250 officers and men of the 1st Dorsets, left Tilbury for Archangel in May of 1919. What had started as a move to keep German submarines from using North Russian ports as bases, had now become part of the last-ditch attempt to stave off bolshevism. But the issue was being decided elsewhere than on that bleak northern seaboard, and British intervention could hardly have affected the outcome even if our White Russian allies had not proved almost as troublesome as the Red enemy. After some fairly futile marching back and forth through forest and marsh, the battalion were not sorry to leave while they still could. They were back in England by October.

The remainder of the 1st Dorsets were by this time in Londonderry, where a not dissimilar revolutionary situation prevailed, and the 'troubles' south of the border were having an unsettling effect to the north of it. 'Aid to the civil power', which invariably includes being the target for stones and bottles, occupied the battalion's energies, and tried their patience pretty thoroughly during the succeeding three years. Londonderry, then as now, contained all the necessary materials for civil conflagration. The worst examples occurred in May and June 1920, when only an armoured car was sufficient to have a sedative effect; and they were quite content to exchange that uneasy island for the less feverish climate of Aldershot in the autumn of 1921, and gratified to be sped on their way by references to their 'intelligence and steadiness', their discipline and good conduct. It was while they were in Ireland that the Regiment lost Colonel C. C. Hannay, one of its most popular officers whose command of the 5th during the war had led it to be known, in the manner of the old Line Regiments, as 'Hannay's Battalion'. After a year at Aldershot, the battalion sailed for Malta.

The 2nd Battalion, which had started the war in India, and ended it in Damascus, returned to India in October 1919 to resume their 'interrupted' foreign tour. India, like Ireland, was a country with unrest always simmering somewhere below the surface—hence the predominance of these two countries in the 'peacetime' history of the British Army—and in 1922 the routine of exercises and ceremonial parades was interrupted by a fresh outbreak of revolt among those incorrigible insurgents, the Moplahs. The cause this time, as distinct from a natural predilection for violence, was Congress Party's agitation for 'Swaraj', or Home Rule; its manifestations the usual ones of looting, terrorisation and the forcible conversion of all and sundry to the Moplah's particular and fanatical brand of Mohammedanism.

When the small local force was overwhelmed, the Dorsets moved in. Within a week they had a hundred or more under siege in a mosque at Tirurangadi, but in the exchange of fire and the subsequent sally, fifty of the Moplahs escaped, and the Dorsets had a dozen casualties. After this the Moplahs split up into a host of small marauding bands, the rain fell in buckets, and the detachments who went squelching through the forests of Malabar after them had a perfectly horrible time. Occasionally they were able to catch up with a party and teach them a lesson: occasionally they were themselves ambushed; and it was in one of these incidents that Lieutenant Harvey—of Kut fame—was killed.

By mid-October so little progress had been made that the Dorsets were reinforced by a number of Gurkha battalions, a major sweep through the disaffected areas was laid on, and the leisurely processes of the civil courts were replaced by martial law. These measures were more successful; and by the time the Dorsets were relieved in November, the Moplahs had lost several hundreds of their numbers in a series of sharp actions, and the revolt was petering out. Of interest was the award to four soldiers of the Battalion of the Empire Gallantry Medal; the holders of this medal had it replaced by the George Cross in 1941. No sooner had the Battalion arrived at Bangalore, however, than fifty of its members were called out to disperse an angry crowd of 8,000, which they succeeded in doing with commendable—and commended—firmness.

Six weeks later they were in the Sudan. Malaria, not politics, was the main anxiety in Khartoum at this time, for a change; but after a mere three months they were moved to Egypt, and in 1924 returned to England. En route they met the 1st Battalion in Malta—an event which had last occurred in India at the time of the amalgamation of the 39th and 54th in 1881, and which one must assume was suitably celebrated.

The uniqueness of the meeting, and the subsequent travels of the 1st Battalion, are a vivid illustration of the realities of Britain's imperial responsibilities at their zenith. Trouble in Egypt spread to Egyptian troops in the Sudan and had the battalion rushing to Moascar on the Canal, and thence to Khartoum and Omdurman where they remained until 1926, when they returned to Malta. From Malta back to India where, for the next six years, they were on call for internal security duties, though they were not, in fact, required in that capacity until the autumn of 1932, when trouble flared up at Dacca, in East Bengal. The weather—like a steam-bath—proved more formidable than the troublemakers; or else the mere presence of the battalion was enough there, as it proved to be in Sialkot three years later, to 'cast a damp' on unruly spirits. At the end of 1936 the battalion was transferred to the Landi Kotal Brigade and the North-West Frontier: here they became expert at mountain warfare—as well as exceedingly fit—but lacked opportunity to use their new skill.*

On January 1, 1938, the 1st Battalion was transformed into a 'rifle battalion', with a headquarters company and four rifle companies. Just over a year later they were back in Malta once more: they were still there when war broke out.

The 2nd Battalion's spell at home was spent, the first three years of it, at Aldershot, and was predictably uneventful. The presentation of new Colours—which now included Shaiba and Ctesiphon among the honours displayed—the restarting of the *Regimental Quarterly*; training; the General Strike; a change of Colonels; these were the highlights of the years 1924–33, interrupted only by a year—the last year, as it turned out—with the occupation forces in Germany, from 1928–29. Their stay was remarkable mainly for the sweeping success of the athletic team. In 1930 the Regiment was linked with the newly completed County Class Cruiser *Dorsetshire*, which from then on adopted the Regimental March as its own; and,

---

* From Landi Kotal they moved to Nowshera where their Brigade Commander was Brigadier the Hon. H. R. L. G. Alexander, later Field-Marshal Lord Alexander of Tunis.

interesting in view of the 1st Battalion's activities later, carried out combined operations against the 'hostile' coastline of the Isle of Wight from their base at Portland.

More like the real thing was the crisis move to Alexandria in 1936, after the Italian invasion of Abyssinia; but our intervention stopped short at sanctions, and in June the battalion moved to Palestine where the Arab rebellion was threatening the entire stability of the country under the British mandate. In that poisoned atmosphere there was no telling who your enemy was; sniping, ambushes, sabotage and a conspiracy of silence among the Arab population made the British soldier's lot both thankless and unpleasant.

For the Dorsets, based first in Jerusalem, then at Jenin, much of the work consisted of escorting convoys, the Jewish buses that ran between Jerusalem and Jaffa being a favourite target for ambushes; and the battalion had an outstanding success in the Bab-el-Wad in July. The operations were notable for co-operation between the three services; and while the Army scoured the Judean hills on foot, the Navy subscribed guns and searchlights, and the RAF provided air support on call from No. 6 Bomber Squadron. It was useful experience, especially for the young soldiers. By the beginning of 1937, the battalion were back in England. In common with the 1st, the 2nd were converted into a rifle battalion; and an increase of motor transport—the 2nd had lost their horses and limbers on leaving for Egypt—and the introduction of the Bren-gun and one anti-tank gun per platoon, were signs, faint but discernible, of the changing technology of war.

1938 and the Munich crisis passed, but by March 1939 tension was building up again, and one result of this was the doubling of the Territorial Army the following month. This chiefly affected the 4th (Territorial) Battalion. With ups and downs, the battalion had managed to survive during the years since the armistice, and by June 1939—an up—

had 1,200 men on its strength. A fortnight before war was declared half of these were detached to form the nucleus of a 'duplicate' battalion which duly became the 5th. Of local interest, the county was divided in half for Territorial purposes, the 4th Battalion having its headquarters at Dorchester and 'representing' Bridport and the northern part of the county, while the 5th was based at Poole and represented the south-eastern part.

The Regiment thus had four battalions in being when war broke out on September 3; and it was not long before one of them was back among the farmsteads and orchards and hopfields of northern France, which had comforted and concealed and occasionally betrayed their fathers before them.

Chapter
13

1939–1945

THE 2nd Battalion, the Dorsetshire Regiment, as part of the 2nd Infantry Division, sailed for France on September 23, 1939. All that stood between them and the German Army, when they took up their position on the Franco-Belgian frontier a week or so later was a ditch with two feet of water in it, and some concrete pill-boxes. But this time there was no Schlieffen Plan—or not yet—and the battalion spent a cold winter improving the defences on their section of the Maginot Line, with the minimum interference from the enemy. It was like being involved in a dream from which, one knew, one must eventually be woken.

The process of awakening began abruptly on April 9, 1940, when the Germans invaded Norway: a month later the blitzkrieg was launched on the Western Front, and by the end of May the BEF was out of France, and France was out of the war.

The retreat to the Channel began, as far as the 2nd Battalion were concerned, on the 16th with a somewhat confused retirement to Brussels. Two days later, near Ghoy, and nine months after war had been declared, they had their first real brush with the enemy. On the 19th they were at Tournai; on the 21st they were out of Belgium altogether; on the 24th they were at Festubert and the situation was crumbling round them, for the Germans had reached Boulogne and were at the gates of Calais and were already pasting the BEF's remaining open port, Dunkirk. On the La Bassée Canal, like the 1st Battalion in 1914 before them, they turned and stood for a brave, forlorn three days. The enemy were all round them and they suffered a steady seep of casualties; then, on the 27th, the Germans launched their final offensive. So stubborn and effective had been their defence that Rommel reported the situation on that day as 'extremely critical'.

'You will hold Festubert unless attacked' Brigade Headquarters signalled the CO, 2nd Dorsets, 'when you will withdraw fighting'. These instructions the battalion obeyed implicitly. The last attack of the day was repulsed that evening; and as the dusk of early summer drew in, the Dorsets—or the 250 of them who had survived—slipped away across country in the wake of the division whose retreat they had been left to cover.

It was a hair-raising night. They were completely surrounded, and only escaped by a route that took them in and out of ditches, through the German lines, across the Béthune-Estaires canal—and back again—to reach Doulieu in the morning and learn, first, that they had been written off for lost, and secondly, that the BEF was being evacuated.

Their last march to the Channel had all the elements of a stunning defeat: lost, ragged and exhausted men, abandoned vehicles and equipment, streams of refugees, almost total breakdown of communications, and overhead, unchallenged German air superiority.

For a further two days the battalion helped to hold the Furnes canal on the Dunkirk perimeter; and then, on the night of May 30, they marched in formation, still with their weapons and under fire, on to the mole and aboard a dredger, which carried them across Channel without disaster and dumped them next morning on Margate pier.

The fiasco of that fine and dreadful summer was over; and one remembers the words of the Dorset officer who wrote of the BEF in 1914: '. . . the old army which had borne the burden and heat of those terrible days . . . had passed away'. Decimated though they were, the Dorsets had survived with honour; and for his leadership which had largely made it possible their CO, Lieutenant-Colonel E. L. Stephenson, was awarded the DSO.

For the next eighteen months the battalion remained in England, mainly on coastal defence in Yorkshire. In the autumn of 1941 they received their sailing orders—which were promptly cancelled; a stroke of luck for the 2nd Division, for the 18th, which went instead, ended up in the bag at Singapore. The battalion did not finally leave the U.K. for India until the spring of 1942.

★

The 1st Battalion were in Malta when the war started; and they too had a year of almost peacetime soldiering. With the 2nd Devons, and regular battalions of the Royal West Kents and Royal Irish Fusiliers, they formed the Malta Brigade, and their job, ostensibly, was the defence of the island. As things turned out, they had other jobs as well. Although the Germans never quite nerved themselves to launch Operation Herkules against Malta any more than Sea Lion against England, from the time Italy entered the war the island was under siege and the threat of invasion, and, for long periods, intensive aerial bombardment. Rommel himself said that the capture of Malta was a prerequisite of victory in North Africa; and the preparation and manning of the coastal defences was one of the basic facts of life in Malta throughout 1941 and '42. As the Navy's control of the sea-routes diminished and the Germans attempted to 'neutralise' the island by saturation bombing, others began to make equal claims on the Army's time, skill and energy—the building of aircraft pens, the manning of light A/A guns, the repairing of runways, and the unloading at top speed of such ships as managed to run the gauntlet of fire through the Narrows.

Major R. T. Gilchrist* writes of this period: 'The year

* In *Malta Strikes Back* (Gale and Polden, 1945).

1942, as far as Malta was concerned, was divided up into two periods. There was the period of bombing and the period of famine.' Intensive bombing—apart from the specific attacks on *Illustrious* in January 1941—started in March 1942, when over 1,000 aircraft came over, in waves of between thirty and seventy, in a single week, and continued through April, when nearly 7,000 tons of bombs rained down on the island. This devastating onslaught, which had the intended effect of temporarily putting a stop to the island's offensive capability, was brought to an end in May when 60 Spitfires, flown in from carriers, destroyed over 200 enemy aircraft in a week; but food, fuel and ammunition were all desperately short. For the garrison and people of Malta, the June and August convoys meant the difference between survival and surrender.

Yet life went on. Training could be carried out without petrol, just as entertainments could be improvised without equipment; and it is recorded that '. . . the Dorsets' strength lay in the organisation of toughening and endurance exercises which they carried out with considerable ingenuity. They constructed the toughest form of obstacle course, combined with battle "inoculation", with exploding bombs, and live ammunition fired for a near miss.' To several of these exercises a full-scale air-raid gave a conclusive verisimilitude.

Siege conditions began to taper off soon after the Battle of Alamein; and in March 1943 231 (1st Malta) Brigade—2nd Devons, 1st Hampshires and 1st Dorsets—sailed from Malta for Alexandria and three months of planning and rehearsal before setting out, at the beginning of July, for the invasion of Sicily.

★

When the 2nd Battalion left England in the *Reina del Pacifico* in April 1942 they hoped they were bound for the Western Desert. Instead they found themselves in India; and it was almost two years before they were in action.

Much of this time was spent in carrying out the most exacting kinds of training that the wit of Major-General J. M. L. Grover could devise. From JEWTs (Jungle Exercises Without Trees) and landing exercises without water, they moved to the tropical forests of southern India; and by the time they left Ahmednagar by rail for Assam they were about as well-prepared for what lay ahead as realistic training could make them. Their spirit is exemplified, perhaps, by the puzzled remark made concerning them by Lieutenant-Colonel Jock MacNaught, on his arrival from England at this time to take command—he couldn't understand it, he said, but 'no one ever seemed to be put on a charge'!

When they arrived at Bokajan in April 1944, the Japanese 'Army of Invasion of India' had just carried off its spectacular three-week, 100-mile advance up the Manipur Road, had invested Imphal and Kohima, and seemed all set to sweep on to capture the arsenal of Dimapur and to cut the Bengal and Assam railway. Within a few days the battalion were on their way to recover Kohima and in action.

The operations against the Japanese-held terraces above the Imphal-Dimapur road and the village of Kohima—operations known as the Battle of Kohima, though the battalion's objectives were, in fact, the District Commissioner's bungalow and tennis court—lasted for the best part of three desperate weeks. During the whole of this siege, for that is what it was, the opposing forces on their separate terraces were less than fifty yards apart: the Japanese well dug in with carefully sited and immensely strong gun positions to sweep virtually every approach line; the British—Dorsets, Royal Welch Fusiliers, Royal Berks, the 4th Rajputs and the Royal West Kents—sniped at and mortared from every angle, and with no option but to attack up the steep terraces into that storm of fire. The spur had been fought over for a month in very hot weather, and now the monsoon had broken; no picture of Kohima is complete without that overpowering stench of putrefying flesh, the flies and the heat and the rain.

In the first attack, on April 26/27, 'A' Company of the battalion, led by Captain H. D. Bowles, slipped past the Japanese positions and dug in close to the DC's bungalow. The bluff now held by A Company commanded the junction of three vital roads, enabling our future attacks to be developed. Here, under annihilating fire, they managed to hang on for a week before being relieved. Only 28 of the original 100 returned.

The only answer was a tank; the problem, which took a fortnight and much sweat to solve, was to get a tank up there and into the right position. This was finally achieved by the sappers on May 12; and the following day it rumbled on to the tennis court terrace and opened up at the Japanese positions at point-blank range, and with the infantry hard behind it, charging through the skeletal trees as the enemy took to their heels. Amazingly, the final assault only cost the Dorsets one man killed and two wounded; but 74 had died during the preceeding nineteen days, in those conditions which General Wood compared to the battlefield of the Somme.

The key to Kohima had been turned; but it was three weeks before the enemy were finally driven off Kohima Ridge and the mountain spurs around it: three weeks of monsoon rains, hard scrambling up and down the streaming hillsides, and a steady drain of casualties. But at the end of it the momentum of the Japanese advance had been turned back upon itself, and the pursuit of them back down the Manipur Road began. On June 18 the battalion, having advanced 16 miles in the day, crossed the frontier into Burma, and thus added 'Primus *ex* Indis' unofficially to the Regiment's honours.

The Battle of Kohima was won. Altogether it had cost the battalion 473 officers and men, killed, wounded, died or sick. On June 27 they arrived in Imphal, in the un-

Kohima Ridge, May 1944—a view across the tennis-court of the District Commissioner's late bungalow.

accustomed luxury of motor transport; and there, with the long, hard, rain-sodden length of Burma ahead of them, we will leave them while we pick up the 1st Battalion on their way to Sicily and the first of their three assault landings.

After a dirty passage, the battalion landed, in a Force-8 gale, at Marzamemi, just north of Cape Passaro, on July 10, 1943, at a quarter to three in the morning. They met with little opposition, and had achieved all their immediate objectives by noon. During the ensuing three weeks they marched and fought their way north-west to the very foothills of Mount Etna—upon a spur of which Agira rose sheer, like a fairy-tale castle, the climax of a tract of steep, mountainous country which was desperately defended at this moment by Panzer Grenadiers whose orders were to hold out to the end. At Agira, and again at Regalbuto a week later, the battalion attacked and overran strong German positions in that steep and stony countryside. 'These Tommies fight well', a German officer confided to his diary. General Leese said much the same thing in a message to the Brigade later: 'Your fights at Agira and

Sergeant W. Evans winning the bar to his MM, near Pizzo, 1943. From the drawing by Bryan de Grineau.
D.R.—8

Regalbuto will ever be an epic in the Regimental Histories
of your Battalions.' But the neatest compliment—and
a clue to Monty's popularity, perhaps—lies in the story
quoted by Lieutenant-Colonel A. E. C. Bredin,* then a
company commander:

> 'Monty made a speech to the Brigade. After compliment-
> ing them on their fine show, he said he hoped to take the
> Brigade with him wherever he went. A bit of a glum look
> went round the ranks. Malta Brigade had been abroad
> longer than most Eighth Army men. Monty was quick
> to notice the reaction and added drily, "Of course, I
> might go to England". The effect was instantaneous.
> Smiles and loud cheers greeted the remark.'

From Sicily the 231st Brigade went on in September to
land in Italy. Their destination was changed twice as the
5th Division, which had landed on the Toe five days earlier,
surged northwards; and the Dorsets finally set foot on the
mainland of Europe near Pizzo on September 8. The
actual landings were a shambles—the first man ashore was
an NCO with the mail—and the battalion ran into
considerable opposition which was not noticeably diminished by the Kittyhawk fighter-bombers that strafed
the wrong side. But it was an odd, equivocal time, for
on the very day of the landings Italy surrendered, which
was confusing enough: the fact that it made no difference
was even more confusing.

After a couple of days of energetic advance, however, the
Malta Brigade was hauled out of the line, and heard that
Monty had been as good as his word—they were going
home. Many of the Dorsets had been abroad for six years
and more, and, as Colonel Bredin remarks, 'the news took
some time to sink in'.

By now, the end of 1943, preparations and training for

---

* In his *Three Assault Landings* (Gale and Polden, 1946).
Brigadier Bredin, DSO, MC, DL, is now (1969) Colonel of the
Devonshire and Dorset Regiment.

1st Dorsets land in Normandy, June 6, 1944—their third assault on an enemy-held coastline inside a year. (A water-proofed carrier landing.)

D-Day were in full swing; and quite soon the battalion, as part of the 50th (Northumbrian) Division, were deeply involved in combined operations exercises, first on the East Coast, then at Inveraray, Studland Bay—which was home ground for them, if not for their Geordie comrades— and Hayling Island. On May 31 the battalion started to embark in the *Empire Spearhead* and *Empire Crossbow*— and this time there was no going back. Ahead lay the beaches of Normandy, and all Germanised Europe through which, quite soon, no less than three Dorset battalions would be fighting their way.

1st Dorsets share with 1st Hampshires the honour of having been the first British troops to land in Normandy; and when the two battalions made their way ashore at Le

Hamel early on the morning of June 6, it was their third assault upon a hostile coast within twelve months, a record which the two regiments claim is unmatched.

Of the three this was by far and away the greatest, not only in its scale but in its power to light up the imagination: a whole world hung in suspense as those first intrepid files plunged ashore and the first machine-guns opened up to meet them. In spite of strong German reactions, however, and a good many casualties, they quickly fought their way inland, captured the stoutly defended Point 54, and by nightfall had achieved all their objectives. One of the most urgent of these had been Arromanches, designated for the construction of the first Mulberry Harbour.

> 'So ended a most memorable day', wrote Colonel Bredin. 'The German defences on the coast had been broken into and through, and very severe casualties had been inflicted on them in men and material.'

But only at the cost of 128 officers and men of the battalion. For the next few days the Dorsets were in the van of the advance in company with 8th Armoured Brigade, with whom they shared the taking and holding of 'Tiger Hill', against the tough and infamous 12th SS Panzer Division, and earned an encomium from the Brigade Commander, who found 'the whole behaviour of the unit exceptional'. During the ensuing week the battalion continued to advance against stiff opposition and through that difficult country of hedgerow and wood which the French call *bocage*; and on June 19, in the neighbourhood of Hottot, south of Bayeux, during very severe fighting, the CO, Lieutenant-Colonel E. A. M. Norrie was mortally wounded, and 100 more of the battalion were killed or wounded.

This was the period when the effects of the great gale, which played such merry hell with the Mulberry Harbour, Port Winston, and the build-up programme, pressed most

Infantry and Anti-Tank guns moving up along a tank track in the Normandy Bocage.

hardly on the jaded troops who had landed on D-Day and had been fighting without respite ever since. There was no doubt now that the Allies were back on the continent to stay; but ahead of them still lay a month of almost static slogging, of small, hard-won advances along the rigorous road to Villers Bocage, which culminated in the destruction of the German 7th and 15th Armies in the Falaise trap. At this time, Montgomery's 21st Army Group had, as planned, drawn to its front virtually the whole of the German armour in Normandy, to allow the US forces to break out round St. Lo.

For the battalion this was a testing time, with a hard stint of patrolling, and some savage fighting in the struggle for the key enemy post of Hottot village. Such normally harmless spots as 'Brigadier's Farm', La Pignerie ('The Piggery'), and Les Landes were dearly bought. On August 4, following the break-out battles which started at the end of

July, they entered what was left of Villers Bocage, and, a week later, came the battalion's final action in Normandy, at St. Pierre-La-Vieille. The two opposing German divisions were defeated and scattered, and, in conjunction with all that was happening elsewhere, the battle for Normandy was won, and the second phase of the invasion complete.

A month before this, at an investiture in the field held by General Montgomery, Colonel Bredin—previously Second-in-Command of the battalion, but since July 8, its CO—was decorated with the MC. Colonel Bredin commanded the 1st Battalion until February (they returned to England in December), and then took over the 5th Battalion before the Rhine crossing.

The 4th and 5th Battalions, both part of the 43rd 'Wessex' Division whose badge was the Wyvern,* had landed at Arromanches in the fourth week of June, and were in action within a few days. The 4th had their first real taste of battle at Eterville as part of the Division's attack on Hill 112—'a model attack'—and took a pasting at Maltot; the 5th had theirs at Chateau de Fontaine, which they captured, and at La Bigne in early August, where, according to the battalion historian, 'Battalion Headquarters was in the unusual position of being able to watch a battle taking place in their rear', and the success of the action caused the Germans to withdraw along their whole front.

After three weeks in the line, the 4th moved back for a rest. 'I shall never forget the sight the men looked', wrote one officer; 'dirty, muddy clothes, and hardly a man had shaved in eight days; but they were all on top of form, they arrived singing popular songs, and all had the usual wisecrack'. That sentence, about men straight out of an

---

* Our oldest (royal) military emblem, it flew above Harold at Hastings, and was borne beside Edward III at Crécy.

Men of the 5th Dorsets, accompanied by a Churchill tank, in action at Horseshoe Wood, July 10, 1944.

extended and gruelling time in action, speaks volumes for the spirit of the Dorsets.

When the break-out came in August, the 43rd Division headed due east for the Seine, and crossed the river at the twin towns of Vernon and Vernonnet on the 27th. Their progress there—and thereafter into Belgium—was in the nature of a triumphal procession, as the liberated and ecstatic villagers and townspeople rushed out to swamp them with flowers, fruit, kisses and wine. Anglo-French relations have never been so cordial, possibly, as during those first few euphoric weeks after Normandy.

With the Seine crossing secure, the Guards Armoured Division passed through to make their famous dash north-east through Picardy and into Belgium, leaving the Division stranded for a fortnight without transport.

Nevertheless, by September 12 they were on the outskirts of Brussels where, according to the 4th Battalion chronicle, a German wine store was discovered which supplied them with champagne for 'breakfast, dinner, tea and supper for many days to come'.

While the 1st Battalion veered off northwards to Antwerp, Merxem (the Regiment had been *there* before—in January 1814) and those two ill-omened waterways, the Albert and Escaut canals, all three battalions became involved—and one, the 4th, achieved a special fame—in Operation 'Market Garden'. This complex and daring attempt to capture the river crossings at Arnhem, Nijmegen, Eindhoven and Grave and so turn the defence-line of the Rhine and cut off 100,000 Germans in Holland, started on September 17; and its epic course has passed into legend. Of that legend, the work of the 4th Dorsets on the night of the 24th and afterwards is an indelible part.

Ordered to cross the Neder Rijn to the south-west of Arnhem and cover the evacuation of the survivors of 1st Airborne, they made their way over under annihilating fire athwart a strong current in foundering boats. About 300 of the battalion made it and held on for thirty-six hours while, with unimaginable difficulty, some 2,400 paratroopers were ferried back. Very few of the 4th, however, made that nightmare return journey; and their desperate courage was specifically acknowledged by Montgomery when he wrote★ :

'I decided to withdraw the gallant Arnhem bridgehead that night . . . During the night of the 25/26 September the withdrawal was carried out in assault boats. The greatest gallantry and skill were shown in this operation, both by detachments operating from north of the river, and by a battalion of 43 Division which assisted them; by 0600 hours on 26th September, when intense enemy fire made further crossings impossible, about 2,400 men of 1 Airborne Division, Polish Parachute Brigade, and

★ In *Normandy to the Baltic* (Hutchinson, London 1947), p. 184.

III

Lt-Colonel A. E. C. Bredin (right) and Major P. H. W. Brind (standing) with leaders of the Dutch Resistance.

4th Battalion the Dorset Regiment had been safely evacuated. Other detachments of the Dorsets were left on the north bank of the river still fighting in a most gallant manner to cover the operation.'*

It was a tough time for everyone involved, whether the 4th and 5th Battalions on the fire-swept banks of the Neder Rijn, or the 1st fighting their way north across 'The Island' between Nijmegen and Arnhem. For a fortnight the Germans did all they knew to destroy the salient; but it held; and for the first time for three months the surging armies of liberation were brought virtually to a standstill. But from that period all three battalions' histories are charted with violent and unforgotten names: the 1st's battles at Heuval and Bemmel, which helped to secure the vital Nijmegen bridgehead*; the 5th's two brilliant actions

* Subsequently, Lieutenant-General Sir Frederick A. M. Browning, KBE, CB, DSO, presented the 4th Battalion with a 1st Airborne flag in remembrance of the part played by the battalion in the relief of the 1st Airborne Division at Arnhem from 24th to 26th September 1944. It is now in the Regimental Museum.

at Bauchem and Dorset Wood in the Sittard triangle, which latter the 4th took over and held for eight miserable days, much of it spent 'digging in and pumping water out of the flooded trenches to the accompaniment of a continuous downpour of shells' (January, 1945).

The 1st Battalion claimed another 'first' about this time: to quote Brigadier Bredin: 'So it came about that a patrol of the 1st Dorsets, consisting of Lieutenant G. D. Walsh, Sergeant Pinfold and Lance-Corporal Davis . . . crossed the German border near Beek at 1635 hours on September 29—the first British Infantry to set foot on Reich territory.'

On December 16 Von Runstedt launched his offensive in the Ardennes; and if conditions in Dorset Wood had been reminiscent of those in 'Plugstreet' Wood in 1915, this, in its short-lived ferocity could be compared with Ludendorff's in March 1918. Both the 4th and 5th Battalions were alerted but not involved: but the 1st had already departed for England, for the 50th Division—'one of the outstanding battle-fighting divisions of the British Army—if not the greatest of them all'—was to utilise all those years of battle-experience in training others.

Once the German counter-offensive had been contained the Allies' assault upon Germany itself could continue; and this meant, first, the elimination of all enemy forces to the west of the Rhine, and the breaching of the Siegfried Line and its outlying defences. The Battle of the Reichswald —'this horrible battle' as General Horrocks called it— began on February 7, and lasted for the better part of a month. Rain, inundations natural and enemy-contrived, mud and determined opposition by eleven German divisions, combined to render it singularly unpleasant. Both battalions were involved at various stages, notably the

---

* Which gained 'Aam' as one of the ten Second World War battle-honours to be borne on the colours. The Honours Committee refused inexplicably to give Bemmel or Heuval!

5th in a difficult night affair at Berghot, and the 4th in a sharp fight near Cleve. It was after this battle that Lieutenant-Colonel Bredin took over command of the 5th Battalion, and was nearly blown up—not for the first time— near Griethausen on the Rhine. By the end of February the Allies were firmly in command of the Rhine approaches; and on March 23 the crossing of the last great natural barrier between them and the German heartland began.

In its strength, its careful preparation, and its use of all the implements of modern war, the crossing of the Rhine was like a repeat of D-Day. Both battalions, following up the initial assault, were over within three days and quickly gained their immediate objectives. Thereafter the speed of advance was like that after the German defeat in Normandy; and the rout of the Wehrmacht—for it was no less—took the Wessex Division, first, back over the border into Holland, where Hengelo was liberated by the 5th Battalion. At Borne—where the town square was renamed Dorset Square after the 4th Battalion—(is it still, one wonders, and if so, what do the children of the post-war generation make of it?)—they swung north-east towards Bremen, after crossing the Dortmund-Ems Canal, and by April 15 were within fifteen miles of the port. Their progress was impeded more by blown-up bridges, mines and road blocks than by their defeated and demoralised enemies; though an occasional desperate remnant gave them trouble: it was accelerated by the use of armoured personnel carriers— converted tanks, or SP gun chassis known as 'defrocked priests'. The war-time A.P.C.s were generally known as 'kangaroos'.

At the beginning of May they were past Bremen and racing out along the peninsula towards Cuxhaven; and it was there, in the village of Augustendorf, that the 4th fought their last skirmish—against a solitary Spandau. The 5th were actually counter-attacked in a small way at Tarmstedt, and had their last exchange of fire at Glinstedt.

Two days later it was all over; and, as the chronicler of the 5th put it rather glumly:

'The Higher Commanders had their impressive ceremonies of surrender* but for the private soldier the war had just fizzled out'.

Thereby catching very accurately the sense of anticlimax which is the ashen fruit of victory.

To round off the story of these two battalions, the 5th remained in Germany as part of the British Army of Occupation, first not far from Hamburg, and later in Berlin, until they were disbanded in the spring of 1946. The 4th, however, after six months in Germany, was transferred to Bari, in the south of Italy, and from there to the 'Morgan Line' on the Trieste border, with the object of preventing Yugoslavians infiltrating into that explosive little enclave. The 4th were put into a temporary state of suspended animation in 1947, to be resuscitated in their old role of Territorial Battalion, in the following year. In 1950 they received their first draft of National Servicemen.

This is as good a moment as any, before we follow the 2nd Battalion's victorious march to Mandalay, to mention briefly the other wartime Dorset battalions. The 6th, which began as a Home Defence unit, later became the 30th and served in a variety of capacities in Sicily and Gibraltar; the 7th and 8th became, in 1941, Light Anti-Aircraft Regiments, RA, were numbered the 110th and the 105th respectively, and served overseas, the former in North-West Europe, the latter in North Africa and Italy; the 9th remained in England as a Training Battalion; and, finally, the 70th was formed and served as a battalion for young soldiers.

★

* The 4th and 5th were in the first victory parade of all, on May 12 at Bremerhaven, where General Horrocks, their Corps Commander (30 Corps) since Normandy, took the salute.

In June 1944, while the Allies were still struggling to gain elbow room in Normandy, the 2nd Battalion were on the road to Imphal. Their CO was now Lieutenant-Colonel O. G. W. White* who had had the battalion for a time during the previous year, and now resumed command on the promotion of Jock McNaught to Brigadier. Before they could continue the drive south into Burma, however, they were called upon to clear the Japanese forces out of Tamu. The conditions were the familiar ones, only more so: dense, jungle-covered mountains; incessant rain, intense cold on the peaks and sultry heat in the valleys; scrub typhus; and large numbers of Japanese, living, dying or dead. Here, as in other places during the advance, many of the enemy were far gone with starvation and disease: 'one did not have to waste ammunition on the Nip: one just grabbed a passing one, shook him and he died'.

After Tamu, the battalion had some months in camp at Maram, north of Imphal; and then, just before Christmas 1944, set out on the hard march from Kalewa, on the Upper Chindwin, to Shwebo, near the Mu. For transport, apart from their feet, they had a number of jeeps, carriers and trucks—including two captured from the Japanese—a water-cart, and some forty mules. Their march took them through the 'dry belt' of upper Burma, and water was short; the days were so hot that most of their movements were made at night, the dust was thick, the road rough and packs enormous; and at Ye-U, on the River Mu, they caught up with the enemy once more.

In a brisk action—'The 54th', wrote Colonel White, 'had seen for themselves, as had their predecessors often in

* Geoffrey White has the Dorsets in his bones, being the son of an old Dorset: 'the Fifty Fourth has been my virtual home', he writes; and his book *Straight on for Tokyo* is an ebullient account of the 2nd's war on which I have drawn deeply for this chapter. The Regimental Museum owes much to him, and he is the Regiment's industrious archivist.

the past, that there are no soldiers in the world who can stand up to the British bayonet'—the force crossed the river, secured the bridgehead, and pressed on to Shwebo, which they entered on January 9.

Their next and greatest obstacle, the Rhine of this campaign, was the Irrawaddy—1,500 yards wide, with a 4-knot current and constantly shifting sandbanks, the Japanese dug in on the far side, and precious few boats, and most of them more or less unhandy. In the event, and apart from the Worcesters who got driven back on their first attempt, the crossing went very well, though it had its anxious moments as the DUKWs invariably broke down where the current would sweep them and their occupants within the enemy's field of fire. But within forty-eight hours the division had cleared Ngazun, and all was set for a concerted drive on Mandalay.

The forty-odd miles, largely cross-country, took the 5th Brigade a fortnight, and 'each battalion had about half-a-dozen actions during this advance'. For the Dorsets specifically this included the very dodgy night-battle for 'Dirty Pagoda' against prepared positions, which, though costing them 62 casualties, was a complete success. On March 17 they were in Ava—which the 54th had failed to reach from Arakan in 1826—and three days later Mandalay had fallen.

The battalion had one final task before it, the assault on the strongly held and easily defensible plateau below Mount Popa. The reduction of this natural fortress took a week, helped by the fact that, as a Burmese headmen reported, 'all the Japanese soldiers have run away to Ywathit village'; but hindered by the fact—from the same source—'that all the roads have with explosive please take carre.' (The note, incidentally, was addressed to 'The Commonder in Chief'.) 'Carre' was duly taken, along with Popa and her equally frivolous-sounding sister-village, Popalon.

The battalion had had over a year of unremitting jungle
warfare with all its concomitants of exhaustion and disease;
they had covered 700 fighting miles, mostly on foot; and
they were due for refit, rest and reorganisation. Behind them
and below, as they flew out in the hard-worked Dakotas of
Air Transport Command, was the foursquare stone
memorial to the Kohima dead, and a multitude of plain
white crosses that marked the graves of all those men of
Dorset who would never leave again those alien hills.

Chapter

14

1945-1958

As at the conclusion of every war in history—one remembers the 39th being nearly 'broke' in 1713— so in the years immediately after 1945, and despite continuing international tensions, the armed forces were cut back. The Dorsets quickly resumed their normal peacetime structure. The first to go were the war service battalions, only the 4th—the old Territorial battalion— being revived in 1948, to survive, and carry the old name, until 1967.

But this time retrenchment and reform were to extend further and bite more deeply than after earlier wars or even Cardwell's reforms. In the end the Regiment was virtually to lose its separate identity, due to amalgamation.

After the disbandment of the war service battalions, the 2nd were the next to feel the axe's edge. After their refit in India, where they still were when the armistice with Japan was concluded in August, they were chosen by General Slim to form part of Force 152—otherwise known as the British Commonwealth Occupation Force, or BCOF —and landed at Kure, on the island of Honshu, in April 1946.

They spent a year among their former enemies, moving from Matsue on the north coast of Honshu* to Gomen on the south coast of Shikoku,* and putting in seven weeks' guard and ceremonial duties in Tokyo. Their spell in the capital happened to coincide with Plassey Day; and on Friday, June 28, 1946, the battalion trooped the Regimental Colour in the courtyard of the Imperial Palace before General Eichelberger, Commander of the

* The two islands of Japan.

HM the Queen meets Old Comrades during her visit to the Regiment, July 3, 1952.

Land Forces in Japan, and a handsome turn-out of top American and British brass.

In Gomen, by contrast, they underwent the traditional Japanese experience of a major earthquake, followed by the traditional tidal wave, and were dragged in, as soldiers always are, to clear up the mess. And everywhere they went they puzzled over the dichotomy of this extraordinary race, with their insensate brutality and their cultured charm. How can any people be at once so courteous, brave and cruel? It was not a question to which they could find any easy answer.

Early in 1947 the British Brigade was withdrawn from Japan, and the battalion moved to Kluang in Malaya, where they had six months of internal security duties, and 'the dreariness of a peacetime garrison life under war-time living conditions', before returning to England to be, under the increasing stringency of the times, 'stood down'.

It was a hard blow to take, but there was no reprieve; and on January 6, 1948, with the privilege of the honorary freedom of Dorchester—bestowed on the Regiment in 1946—they marched bravely through the town with bayonets fixed and Colours flying, to hand over those same Colours to the Lord Lieutenant of the County on the Depot Square. So ended the story of the 2nd Battalion, the Dorset Regiment, formerly the 54th Regiment of Foot.

Seventeen months later the 1st Battalion, which moved to Austria in 1948, also lost its identity when, together with a cadre of the old 2nd Battalion, at a formal amalgamation parade in Vienna, a new 1st Battalion (39th and 54th) was created. Two years later the Royal Assent was granted the Dorsetshire Regiment to style itself the Dorset Regiment, a patronymic hitherto reserved for purposes of abbreviation only. In this way the Regiment, at the urgent request of those interested in the correctness of place names and titles, abandoned a style by which the County Regiment had been known since 1807 and the County Class Ship of the Line had been known for some hundred or more years before that.

The Colonel from 1933 to 1946 was the distinguished soldier and administrator of the Sudan, General Sir Hubert Huddleston. He was succeeded in 1946 by Brigadier Charles Woodhouse, who 'had fought our machine-guns in 1914', and commanded the 2nd Battalion in Palestine in 1936; his and the Dorsets' memorial being the regimental cottages built for men of the Dorsets and their families—perhaps the warmest-hearted way of remembering a regiment's dead. In 1952, Major-General George Wood, whose name has appeared earlier in this chronicle, took over from Brigadier Woodhouse.

The 1st Battalion, after their stint with the training

HRH Princess Marina, Colonel-in-Chief of the Dorset Regiment, with the Colonel, Major-General G. N. Wood, during a visit in 1954. Princess Marina had just been presented with the Regimental brooch which she is wearing.

division, returned to Germany in the spring of 1946, shifting about the country, and, like the 2nd, putting in a spell of duty in an enemy capital, Berlin. In 1952 they were in Vienna, and there they celebrated the 250th anniversary of the raising of the 39th; while back home, HM The

Queen visited the Regimental Depot at Dorchester. At her coronation—after the battalion's transfer from Austria to Hong Kong—HRH Princess Marina, Duchess of Kent, was appointed Colonel-in-Chief of the Regiment. This was a tremendously popular appointment. General Wood, who remained Colonel until 1962, writes of her 'as a wonderful friend, who never missed a regimental function, and whose unique gaiety and sense of fun were a constant delight'. Princess Marina continued her colonelcy on amalgamation, until her death.

From Hong Kong the Battalion moved, in 1953, to Korea, where they served under the aegis of the United Nations; but the truce was in force during the eleven

The Keep, Dorchester. Built in 1879, it was for almost 80 years the entrance to the Regimental Depot. Today it houses the Dorset Military Museum and part of RHQ, the Devonshire and Dorset Regiment.

months they were there and, though they got very cold, and, incidentally, celebrated the 54th's 200th anniversary in, to quote Colonel White, 'very jungly conditions', they saw no action.

In 1954 they returned once more, and for the last time, to Germany; and at Minden, in that country, on May 21, 1958, the 1st Battalion, the Dorset Regiment was amalgamated with the Devonshire Regiment (the old 11th) to form the Devonshire and Dorset Regiment. Another link with the past was broken, or another link with the future forged, depending upon which way one chose to look at it.

As far as the past is concerned, the sense of loss and waste among the old members of the Regiment is very strong. A good county regiment was so many more things than an efficient fighting formation: it was a focus for a loyalty at once proud and affectionate, and had something of the closed familiarity, the jealousy for its own reputation, and the concern for its members, of a family. This is exemplified in the Dorsets by the strength and cohesion of the Old Comrades Association: its symbol is the Keep at Dorchester, with its excellent museum, which draws nearly 20,000 visitors a year.

As for the future, the ties are still strong, even though their *raison d'être* has been modified. As Brigadier Bredin himself says: 'Our aim is to maintain the entity of the regimental family within the Prince of Wales's Division to which it now belongs'.

The Regimental March

THE Regimental March is an adaptation of a popular seventeenth-century song, 'The Maid of Glenconnel', otherwise known as 'The Pearl of the Fountain'. It is said to have been the favourite ditty of the wife of John Campbell—later the fifth Duke of Argyll—who raised the 54th Regiment in 1755, and was played so often that it became the Regiment's Quick Step. In 1881, when the 39th and 54th were amalgamated to become the 1st and 2nd Battalions, it was adopted as the Regimental March of the Dorsets.

Some Notable Dates in the History of The Dorset Regiment

1702	39th raised by Colonel Richard Coote.
1755	54th raised by Lieutenant-Colonel John Campbell.
1757	June 23: Battle of Plassey. Three companies of 39th in action. 'Plassey Day' celebrated ever since.
1779–83	39th in Gibraltar during The Great Siege.
1801	54th at Aboukir Bay, and capture of Fort Marabout.
1803	2/39th raised, with Colonel The Hon. Robert O'Callaghan as CO.
1807	39th's connection with Dorset established.
1811	2/39th at Battle of Albuhera.
1813	1/39th at Vittoria.
1824–26	1st Burma War: 54th in Arakan.
1825–32	39th in Australia. Captain Charles Sturt's journeys of exploration.
1857	November 11: Troopship *Sarah Sands* on fire in Indian Ocean with part of 54th on board. *Sarah Sands* Day celebrated ever since.
1881	39th and 54th amalgamated to form 1st and 2nd Battalions the Dorsetshire Regiment.
1900	2nd Battalion distinguishes itself at Alleman's Nek.
1907	Dorsets complement established at two regular battalions, 3rd (Special Reserve) and 4th (Territorial).
1914–18	During First World War twelve battalions fought in France, Gallipoli, Mesopotamia and Palestine, from Mons onwards.

1916   2nd Battalion captured on fall of Kut-el-Amara (only 70 out of 350 survived subsequent captivity), after the victories of Shaiba, Kut and Ctesiphon.

1939–45   During Second World War nine battalions fought in France ('39–40), Malta, Sicily, Italy, Burma, and Normandy to the Baltic.

1943–44   1st Battalion carry out three assault landings in a row: Sicily, Italy—and first ashore on D-Day.

1944   2nd Battalion at Kohima.

1944   4th Battalion cover retirement of 1st Airborne at Arnhem.

1946–47   2nd Battalion form part of BCOF in Japan.

1949   2nd Battalion merged with 1st Battalion.

1951   Title changed to The Dorset Regiment.

1953   HRH Princess Marina appointed Colonel-in-Chief.

1958   May 21: Regiment amalgamated with Devons to form the Devonshire and Dorset Regiment.